First Workshop on Algorithms and Resources for Modelling of Dialects and Language Varieties 2011

(DIALECTS 2011)

Held at EMNLP 2011

Edinburgh, Scotland, UK
31 July 2011

ISBN: 978-1-61839-247-3

Printed from e-media with permission by:

Curran Associates, Inc.
57 Morehouse Lane
Red Hook, NY 12571

Some format issues inherent in the e-media version may also appear in this print version.

Printed by Curran Associates, Inc. (2011)

For permission requests, please contact the Association for Computational Linguistics at the address below.

Association for Computational Linguistics
209 N. Eighth Street
Stroudsburg, Pennsylvania 18360

Phone: 1-570-476-8006
Fax: 1-570-476-0860

acl@aclweb.org

Additional copies of this publication are available from:

Curran Associates, Inc.
57 Morehouse Lane
Red Hook, NY 12571 USA
Phone: 845-758-0400
Fax: 845-758-2634
Email: curran@proceedings.com
Web: www.proceedings.com

Introduction

Language varieties (and specifically dialects) are a primary means of expressing a person's social affiliation and identity. Hence, computer systems that can adapt to the user by displaying a familiar socio-cultural identity are expected to raise the acceptance within certain contexts and target groups dramatically. Although the currently prevailing statistical paradigm has made possible major achievements in many areas of natural language processing, the applicability of the available methods is generally limited to major languages / standard varieties, to the exclusion of dialects or varieties that substantially differ from the standard.

While there are considerable initiatives dealing with the development of language resources for minor languages, and also reliable methods to handle accents of a given language, i.e., for applications like speech synthesis or recognition, the situation for dialects still calls for novel approaches, methods and techniques to overcome or circumvent the problem of data scarcity, but also to enhance and strengthen the standing that language varieties and dialects have in natural language processing technologies, as well as in interaction technologies that build upon the former.

What made us think that a such a workshop would be a fruitful enterprise was our conviction that only joint efforts of researchers with expertise in various disciplines can bring about progress in this field. We therefore aimed in our call to invite and bring together colleagues that deal with topics ranging from machine learning algorithms and active learning, machine translation between language varieties or dialects, speech synthesis and recognition, to issues of orthography, annotation and linguistic modelling.

The 2011 Workshop on Algorithms and Resources for Modelling of Dialects and Language Varieties (DIALECTS 2011) is the first workshop to be held on this rather interdisciplinary topic. The workshop received seventeen submissions, out of which six were accepted as oral presentations (long papers) and three as posters (short papers). These papers represent interesting work from almost all the scientific fields that were mentioned in the call as being necessary to contribute to the common goal.

In addition to the submitted papers we are happy to welcome Burr Settles as our invited speaker to give a keynote talk on the topic of using multiple machine learning strategies to facilitate rapid development of NLP tools for new/rare languages/dialects. We hope that this gathering and the proceedings will help to promote and to advance the topic this workshop is centered around. We would like to thank all the authors who submitted their work for consideration. We are also especially grateful to the members of the program committee and the additional reviewers for their insightful and detailed reviews.

Jeremy Jancsary, Friedrich Neubarth, and Harald Trost

Workshop Organizers

Organizers:

Jeremy Jancsary (OFAI, Vienna, Austria)
Friedrich Neubarth (OFAI, Vienna, Austria)
Harald Trost (Medical University Vienna, Austria)

Program Committee:

Gérard Bailly (GIPSA-LAB, CNRS Grenoble, France)
Nick Campbell (CLCS, Trinity College Dublin, Ireland)
Martine Grice (IfL, Phonetik Köln, Germany)
Gholamreza Haffari (BC Cancer Research Center, Vancouver, Canada)
Inmaculada Hernaez Rioja (Univ. of the Basque Country UPV/EHU, Spain)
Philipp Koehn (ILCC, Univ. of Edinburgh, UK)
Michael Pucher (ftw, Vienna, Austria)
Milan Rusko (SAS, Slovak Academy of Sciences, Slovakia)
Kevin Scannell (Dept. of Mathematics and Computer Science, Saint Louis Univ., USA)
Yves Scherrer (LATL, Université de Genève, Switzerland)
Beat Siebenhaar (Institut für Germanistik, Univ. of Leipzig, Germany)

Additional Reviewers:

Johannes Matiasek (OFAI, Vienna, Austria)
Gerard de Melo (Max-Planck-Inst. f. Informatik, Germany/Microsoft Research Cambridge, UK)
Eva Navas Cordón (Univ. of the Basque Country UPV/EHU, Spain)

Invited Speaker:

Burr Settles (Carnegie Mellon University, USA)

Table of Contents

Conference Program

Sunday, July 31, 2011

09:00–09:10 Opening

09:10–10:10 Invited talk by Burr Settles: "Combining Learning Strategies to Make the Most of Language Resources"

10:10–10:30 Open discussion

10:30–11:00 coffee break

11:00–11:30 *Dialect Translation: Integrating Bayesian Co-segmentation Models with Pivot-based SMT*
Michael Paul, Andrew Finch, Paul R. Dixon and Eiichiro Sumita

11:30–12:00 *Dialectal to Standard Arabic Paraphrasing to Improve Arabic-English Statistical Machine Translation*
Wael Salloum and Nizar Habash

12:00–12:30 *PaddyWaC: A Minimally-Supervised Web-Corpus of Hiberno-English*
Brian Murphy and Egon W. Stemle

12:30–14:00 lunch break

14:00–14:40 Poster flash and presentation

14:40–15:10 *Syntactic transformations for Swiss German dialects*
Yves Scherrer

15:10–15:40 *Learning word-level dialectal variation as phonological replacement rules using a limited parallel corpus*
Mans Hulden, Iñaki Alegria, Izaskun Etxeberria and Montse Maritxalar

15:40–16:10 coffee break

16:10–16:40 *Modeling of Stylistic Variation in Social Media with Stretchy Patterns*
Philip Gianfortoni, David Adamson and Carolyn P. Rosé

16:40–17:00 Final discussion

Sunday, July 31, 2011 (continued)

Poster presentations:

Adapting Slovak ASR for native Germans speaking Slovak
Štefan Beňuš, Miloš Cerňak, Sakhia Darjaa, Milan Rusko and Marián Trnka

Phone set selection for HMM-based dialect speech synthesis
Michael Pucher, Nadja Kerschhofer-Puhalo and Dietmar Schabus

WordNet.PT global – Extending WordNet.PT to Portuguese varieties
Palmira Marrafa, Raquel Amaro and Sara Mendes

Dialect Translation:
Integrating Bayesian Co-segmentation Models with Pivot-based SMT

Michael Paul and Andrew Finch and Paul R. Dixon and Eiichiro Sumita
National Institute of Information and Communications Technology
MASTAR Project
Kyoto, Japan
michael.paul@nict.go.jp

Abstract

Recent research on multilingual statistical machine translation (SMT) focuses on the usage of *pivot languages* in order to overcome resource limitations for certain language pairs. This paper proposes a new method to translate a *dialect* language into a foreign language by integrating transliteration approaches based on Bayesian co-segmentation (BCS) models with pivot-based SMT approaches. The advantages of the proposed method with respect to standard SMT approaches are three fold: (1) it uses a standard language as the pivot language and acquires knowledge about the relation between dialects and the standard language automatically, (2) it reduces the translation task complexity by using monotone decoding techniques, (3) it reduces the number of features in the log-linear model that have to be estimated from bilingual data. Experimental results translating four Japanese dialects (Kumamoto, Kyoto, Okinawa, Osaka) into four Indo-European languages (English, German, Russian, Hindi) and two Asian languages (Chinese, Korean) revealed that the proposed method improves the translation quality of dialect translation tasks and outperforms standard pivot translation approaches concatenating SMT engines for the majority of the investigated language pairs.

1 Introduction

The translation quality of SMT approaches heavily depends on the amount and coverage of the bilingual language resources available to train the statistical models. There are several data collection initiatives[1] amassing and distributing large amounts of textual data. For frequently used language pairs like *French-English*, large-sized text data sets are readily available. However, for less frequently used language pairs, only a limited amount of bilingual resources are available, if any at all.

In order to overcome language resource limitations, recent research on multilingual SMT focuses on the use of *pivot languages* (de Gispert and Marino, 2006; Utiyama and Isahara, 2007; Wu and Wang, 2007; Bertoldi et al., 2008; Koehn et al., 2009). Instead of a direct translation between two languages where only a limited amount of bilingual resources is available, the *pivot translation* approach makes use of a third language that is more appropriate due to the availability of more bilingual corpora and/or its relatedness to the source/target language. In most of the previous research, *English* has been the pivot language of choice due to the richness of available language resources. However, recent research on pivot translation has shown that the usage of non-English pivot languages can improve translation quality of certain language pairs, especially when translating from or into Asian languages (Paul et al., 2009).

This paper focuses on the translation of *dialects*, i.e., a variety of a language that is characteristic of a particular group of the language's speakers, into a foreign language. A *standard dialect* (or *standard language*) is a dialect that is recognized as the "correct" spoken and written form of the language. Dialects typically differ in terms of morphology, vocabulary and pronunciation. Various

[1] LDC: http://www.ldc.upenn.edu, ELRA: http://www.elra.info

Proceedings of EMNLP 2011, Conference on Empirical Methods in Natural Language Processing, pages 1–9,
Edinburgh, Scotland, UK, July 27–31, 2011.

methods have been proposed to measure relatedness between dialects using phonetic distance measures (Nerbonne and Heeringa, 1997), string distance algorithms (Heeringa et al., 2006; Scherrer, 2007), or statistical models (Chitturi and Hansen, 2008).

Concerning data-driven natural language processing (NLP) applications like machine translation (MT), however, linguistic resources and tools usually are available for the standard language, but not for dialects. In order to create dialect language resources, previous research utilized explicit knowledge about the relation between the standard language and the dialect using rule-based and statistical models (Habash et al., 2005; Sawaf, 2010). In addition, applying the linguistic tools for the standard language to dialect resources is often insufficient. For example, the task of *word segmentation*, i.e., the identification of word boundaries in continuous text, is one of the fundamental preprocessing steps of MT applications. In contrast to Indo-European languages like English, many Asian languages like Japanese do not use a whitespace character to separate meaningful word units. However, the application of a linguistically motivated standard language word segmentation tool to a dialect corpus results in a poor segmentation quality due to morphological differences in verbs and adjectives, thus resulting in a lower translation quality for SMT systems that acquire the translation knowledge automatically from a parallel text corpus (Paul et al., 2011).

This paper differs from previous research in the following aspects:

- it reduces the data sparseness problem of direct translation approaches by translating a resource-limited dialect language into a foreign language by using the resource-rich standard language as the pivot language.
- it is language independent and acquires knowledge about the relation between the standard language and the dialect automatically.
- it avoids segmentation mismatches between the input and the translation model by mapping the characterized dialect language, i.e., each character is treated as a single token, to the word segmentation of the standard language using a Bayesian co-segmentation model.
- it reduces the translation task complexity by using monotone decoding techniques.
- it reduces the number of features in the log-linear model that have to be estimated from bilingual data.

The details of the proposed dialect translation method are described in Section 2. Experiments were carried out for the translation of four Japanese dialects (Kumamoto, Kyoto, Okinawa, Osaka) into four Indo-European languages (English, German, Russian, Hindi) and two Asian languages (Chinese, Korean). The utilized language resources and the outline of the experiments are summarized in Section 3. The results reveal that the integration of Bayesian co-segmentation models with pivot-based SMT improves the translation quality of dialect to foreign language translation tasks and that the proposed system outperforms standard pivot translation approaches concatenating SMT engines that translate the dialect into the standard language and the standard language MT output into the foreign language for the majority of the investigated language pairs.

2 Dialect Translation

Spoken language translation technologies attempt to bridge the language barriers between people with different native languages who each want to engage in conversation by using their mother-tongue. For standard languages, multilingual speech translation services like the *VoiceTra*[2] system for travel conversations are readily available. However, such technologies are not capable of dealing with dialect languages due to the lack of language resources and the high development costs of building speech translation components for a large number of dialect variations.

In order to reduce such problems, the dialect translation method proposed in this paper integrates two different methods of transducing a given dialect input sentence into a foreign language. In the first step, the close relationship between the local and standard language is exploited to directly map character sequences in the dialect input to word segments in the standard language using a Bayesian co-

[2]http://mastar.jp/translation/voicetra-en.html

segmentation approach, details of which are given in Section 2.1. The proposed transliteration method is described in Section 2.2. The advantages of the proposed Bayesian co-segmentation approach are two fold: it reduces the translation complexity and it avoids segmentation inconsistencies between the input and the translation models. In the second step, a state-of-the-art phrase-based SMT system trained on a large amount of bilingual data is applied to obtain high-quality foreign language translations as described in Section 2.3.

2.1 Bayesian Co-segmentation

The method for mapping the dialect sentences into the standard language word segments is a direct character-to-character mapping between the languages. This process is known as *transliteration*. Many transliteration methods have previously been proposed, including methods based on string-similarity measures between character sequences (Noeman and Madkour, 2010) or generation-based models (Lee and Chang, 2003; Tsuji and Kageura, 2006; Jiampojamarn et al., 2010).

In this paper, we use a generative Bayesian model similar to the one from (DeNero et al., 2008) which offers several benefits over standard transliteration techniques: (1) the technique has the ability to train models whilst avoiding over-fitting the data, (2) compact models that have only a small number of well-chosen parameters are constructed, (3) the underlying generative transliteration model is based on the joint source-channel model (Li et al., 2004), and (4) the model is symmetric with respect to source and target language. Intuitively, the model has two basic components: a model for generating an outcome that has already been generated at least once before, and a second model that assigns a probability to an outcome that has not yet been produced. Ideally, to encourage the re-use of model parameters, the probability of generating a novel bilingual sequence pair should be considerably lower then the probability of generating a previously observed sequence pair. The probability distribution over these bilingual sequence pairs (including an infinite number of unseen pairs) can be learned directly from unlabeled data by Bayesian inference of the hidden co-segmentation of the corpus.

The co-segmentation process is driven by a Dirichlet process, which is a stochastic process defined over a set S (in our case, the set of all possible bilingual sequence pairs) whose sample path is a probability distribution on S. The underlying stochastic process for the generation of a corpus composed of bilingual phrase pairs $(\mathbf{s}_k,\mathbf{t}_k)$ can be written in the following form:

$$\begin{aligned} G|_{\alpha,G_0} &\sim DP(\alpha, G_0) \\ (\mathbf{s}_k,\mathbf{t}_k)|G &\sim G \end{aligned} \tag{1}$$

G is a discrete probability distribution over all the bilingual sequence pairs according to a *Dirichlet process prior* with a *base measure* G_0 and concentration parameter α. The concentration parameter $\alpha > 0$ controls the variance of G; intuitively, the larger α is, the more similar G_0 will be to G.

For the *base measure* that controls the generation of novel sequence pairs, we use a joint spelling model that assigns probability to new sequence pairs according to the following joint distribution:

$$\begin{aligned} G_0((\mathbf{s},\mathbf{t})) &= p(|\mathbf{s}|)p(\mathbf{s}||\mathbf{s}|) \times p(|\mathbf{t}|)p(\mathbf{t}||\mathbf{t}|) \\ &= \frac{\lambda_s^{|\mathbf{s}|}}{|\mathbf{s}|!}e^{-\lambda_s}v_s^{-|\mathbf{s}|} \times \frac{\lambda_t^{|\mathbf{t}|}}{|\mathbf{t}|!}e^{-\lambda_t}v_t^{-|\mathbf{t}|} \end{aligned} \tag{2}$$

where $|\mathbf{s}|$ and $|\mathbf{t}|$ are the length in characters of the source and target sides of the bilingual sequence pair; v_s and v_t are the vocabulary sizes of the source and target languages respectively; and λ_s and λ_t are the expected lengths[3] of the source and target.

According to this model, source and target sequences are generated independently: in each case the sequence length is chosen from a Poisson distribution, and then the sequence itself is generated given the length. Note that this model is able to assign a probability to arbitrary bilingual sequence pairs of any length in the source and target sequence, but favors shorter sequences in both.

The generative model is given in Equation 3. The equation assigns a probability to the kth bilingual sequence pair $(\mathbf{s}_k,\mathbf{t}_k)$ in a derivation of the corpus, given all of the other sequence pairs in the history so far $(\mathbf{s}_{-k},\mathbf{t}_{-k})$. Here $-k$ is read as: "up to but not including k".

$$\begin{aligned} &p((\mathbf{s}_k,\mathbf{t}_k))|(\mathbf{s}_{-k},\mathbf{t}_{-k})) \\ &\qquad = \frac{N((\mathbf{s}_k,\mathbf{t}_k)) + \alpha G_0((\mathbf{s}_k,\mathbf{t}_k))}{N+\alpha} \end{aligned} \tag{3}$$

[3]Following (Xu et al., 2008), we assign the parameters λ_s, λ_t and α, the values 2, 2 and 0.3 respectively.

Input: Random initial corpus segmentation
Output: Unsupervised co-segmentation of the corpus according to the model
foreach *iter=1 to NumIterations* **do**
  foreach *bilingual word-pair* $w \in randperm(\mathcal{W})$ **do**
    foreach *co-segmentation* γ_i *of* w **do**
      Compute probability $p(\gamma_i|h)$
      where h is the set of data (excluding w) and its hidden co-segmentation
    end
    Sample a co-segmentation γ_i from the distribution $p(\gamma_i|h)$
    Update counts
  end
end

Algorithm 1: Blocked Gibbs Sampling

In this equation, N is the total number of bilingual sequence pairs generated so far and $N((\mathbf{s}_k, \mathbf{t}_k))$ is the number of times the sequence pair $(\mathbf{s}_k, \mathbf{t}_k)$ has occurred in the history. G_0 and α are the base measure and concentration parameter as before.

We used a blocked version of a Gibbs sampler for training, which is similar to that of (Mochihashi et al., 2009). We extended their forward filtering / backward sampling (FFBS) dynamic programing algorithm in order to deal with bilingual segmentations (see Algorithm 1). We found our sampler converged rapidly without annealing. The number of iterations was set by hand after observing the convergence behavior of the algorithm in pilot experiments. We used a value of 75 iterations through the corpus in all experiments reported in this paper. For more details on the Bayesian co-segmentation process, please refer to (Finch and Sumita, 2010).

2.2 Dialect to Standard Language Transduction

A Bayesian segmentation model is utilized to transform unseen dialect sentences into the word segmentation of the standard language by using the joint-source channel framework proposed by (Li et al., 2004). The joint-source channel model, also called the *n-gram transliteration model*, is a joint probability model that captures information on how the source and target sentences can be generated simultaneously using transliteration pairs, i.e., the most likely sequence of source characters and target words according to a joint language model built from the co-segmentation from the Bayesian model.

Suppose that we have a dialect sentence $\sigma = l_1 l_2 \ldots l_L$ and a standard language sentence $\omega = s_1 s_2 \ldots s_S$ where l_i are dialect characters, s_j are word tokens of the standard language, and there exists an alignment $\gamma = < l_1 \ldots l_q, s_1 >, \ldots, < l_r \ldots l_L, s_S >$, $1 \leq q < r \leq L$ of K transliteration units. Then, an n-gram transliteration model is defined as the transliteration probability of a transliteration pair $< l, s >_k$ depending on its immediate n preceding transliteration pairs:

$$P(\sigma, \omega, \gamma) = \prod_{k=1}^{K} P(< l, s >_k | < l, s >_{k-n+1}^{k-1}) \quad (4)$$

For the experiments reported in this paper, we implemented the joint-source channel model approach as a weighted finite state transducer (FST) using the *OpenFst* toolkit (Allauzen et al., 2007). The FST takes the sequence of dialect characters as its input and outputs the co-segmented bilingual segments from which the standard language segments are extracted.

2.3 Pivot-based SMT

Recent research on speech translation focuses on corpus-based approaches, and in particular on statistical machine translation (SMT), which is a machine translation paradigm where translations are generated on the basis of statistical models whose parameters are derived from the analysis of bilingual text corpora. SMT formulates the problem of translating a source language sentence src into a target language sentence trg as a maximization problem of the conditional probability:

$$argmax_{trg}\; p(src|trg) * p(trg) \quad (5)$$

where $p(src|trg)$ is called a *translation model* (TM) and represents the generation probability from trg into src, and $p(trg)$ is called a *language model* (LM) and represents the likelihood of the target language (Brown et al., 1993). During the translation process (*decoding*), a score based on the statistical model probabilities is assigned to each translation hypothesis and the one that gives the highest probability is selected as the best translation.

The translation quality of SMT approaches heavily depends on the amount and coverage of the bilingual language resources available to train the statistical models. In the context of dialect translation, where only few bilingual language resources (if any at all) are available for the dialect and the foreign language, only a relatively low translation quality can be obtained. In order to obtain better translations, we apply a pivot translation approach. *Pivot translation* is the translation from a source language (SRC) to a target language (TRG) through an intermediate *pivot* (or *bridging*) *language* (PVT). In this paper, we select the standard language as the pivot language.

Within the SMT framework, various coupling strategies like *cascading*, *phrase-table composition*, or *pseudo-corpus generation* have been proposed. For the experiments reported in this paper, we utilized the *cascading* approach because it is computational less expensive, but still performs comparably well compared to the other pivot translation approaches. In the first step, the dialect input is transcribed into the standard language as described in Section 2.1. Next, the obtained standard language MT output is translated into the target language using SMT models trained on the much larger language resources.

3 Experiments

The effects of integrating Bayesian co-segmentation models with pivot-based SMT are investigated using the *Basic Travel Expressions Corpus* (BTEC), which is a collection of sentences that bilingual travel experts consider useful for people traveling abroad (Kikui et al., 2006). For the dialect translation experiments, we selected Japanese (ja), a language that does not naturally separate word units, and the dialects from the Kumamoto (ja_{ku}), Kyoto (ja_{ky}), Okinawa (ja_{ok}), and Osaka (ja_{os}) areas. All dialects share the same Japanese writing system that combines logographic Chinese characters and two syllabic scripts, i.e., *hiragana* (used for native Japanese words) and *katakana* (used for foreign loanwords or onomatopoeia). For the target language, we investigated four Indo-European languages, i.e., English (en), German (de), Russian (ru), and Hindi (hi) and two Asian languages, i.e., Chinese (zh) and Korean (ko). The corpus statistics are summarized in Table 1, where *Voc* specifies the vocabulary size and *Len* the average sentence length of the respective data sets. These languages differ largely

Table 1: Language Resources

Language		Voc	Len	Order	Unit	Infl
Japanese	ja	17,168	8.5	SOV	none	moderate
English	en	15,390	7.5	SVO	word	moderate
German	de	25,716	7.1	SVO	word	high
Russian	ru	36,199	6.4	SVO	word	high
Hindi	hi	33,629	7.8	SOV	word	high
Chinese	zh	13,343	6.8	SVO	none	light
Korean	ko	17,246	8.1	SOV	phrase	moderate

in word order (*Order*: subject-object-verb (*SOV*), subject-verb-object (SVO)), segmentation unit (*Unit*: phrase, word, none), and degree of inflection (*Infl*: high, moderate, light). Concerning word segmentation, the corpora were preprocessed using language-specific word segmentation tools that are widely-accepted within the MT community for languages that do not use white spaces to separate word/phrase tokens, i.e., CHASEN[4] for Japanese and ICTCLAS[5] for Chinese. For all other languages, simple tokenization tools were applied. All data sets were case-sensitive with punctuation marks preserved.

The language resources were randomly split into three subsets for the evaluation of translation quality (*eval*, 1k sentences), the tuning of the SMT model weights (*dev*, 1k sentences) and the training of the statistical models (*train*, 160k sentences). For the dialect languages, a subset of 20k sentences was used for the training of translation models for all of the resource-limited language pairs. In order to avoid word segmentation errors from the standard language segmentation tool beeing applied to dialect resources, these models are trained on bitext, where the local dialect source sentence is characterized and the target language is segmented using language-specific segmentation tools.

For the training of the SMT models, standard word alignment (Och and Ney, 2003) and language modeling (Stolcke, 2002) tools were used. Minimum error rate training (MERT) was used to tune the decoder's parameters on the *dev* set using the technique proposed in (Och and Ney, 2003). For the translation, an inhouse multi-stack phrase-based decoder was used. For the evaluation of translation quality, we applied the standard automatic evaluation metric

[4]http://chasen-legacy.sourceforge.jp

[5]http://www.nlp.org.cn

Table 2: SMT-based Direct Translation Quality

BLEU (%)

SRC / TRG	ja (160k)	ja (20k)	ja_{ku} (20k)	ja_{ky} (20k)	ja_{ok} (20k)	ja_{os} (20k)
en	56.51	32.84	32.27	31.81	30.99	31.97
de	51.73	26.24	25.06	25.71	24.37	25.18
ru	50.34	23.67	23.12	23.19	22.30	22.07
hi	49.99	21.10	20.46	20.40	19.72	20.96
zh	48.59	33.80	32.72	33.15	32.66	32.96
ko	64.52	53.31	52.93	51.24	49.40	51.57

Table 3: SMT-based Pivot Translation Quality

BLEU (%)

SRC / TRG	ja_{ku}	ja_{ky}	ja_{ok}	ja_{os}
	(SMT$_{SRC\rightarrow ja}$+SMT$_{ja\rightarrow TRG}$)			
en	52.10	50.66	45.54	49.50
de	47.51	46.33	39.42	44.82
ru	44.59	43.83	38.25	42.87
hi	45.89	44.01	36.87	42.95
zh	45.14	44.26	40.96	44.20
ko	60.76	59.67	55.59	58.62

BLEU, which calculates the geometric mean of n-gram precision by the system output with respect to reference translations with the addition of a brevity penalty to punish short sentences. Scores range between 0 (worst) and 1 (best) (Papineni et al., 2002). For the experiments reported here, single translation references were used.

3.1 Direct Translation

Table 2 summarizes the translation performance of the SMT engines used to directly translate the source language dialects into the foreign language. For the large training data condition (160k), the highest BLEU scores are obtained for the translation of Japanese into Korean followed by English, German, Russian, and Hindi with Chinese seeming to be the most difficult translation task out of the investigated target languages. For the standard language (ja), the translation quality for the small data condition (20k) that corresponds to the language resources used for the translation of the dialect languages is also given. For the Asian target languages, gains of $11\%\sim14\%$ BLEU points are obtained when increasing the training data size from 20k to 160k. However, an even larger increase ($24\%\sim27\%$ BLEU points) in translation quality can be seen for all Indo-European target languages. Therefore, larger gains are to be expected when the pivot translation framework is applied to the translation of dialect languages into Indo-European languages compared to Asian target languages. Comparing the evaluation results for the small training data condition, the highest scores are achieved for the standard language for all target languages, indicating the difficulty in translating the dialects. Moreover, the Kumamoto dialect seems to be the easiest task, followed by the Kyoto dialect and the Osaka dialect. The lowest BLEU scores were obtained for the translation of the Okinawa dialect.

3.2 SMT-based Pivot Translation

The SMT engines of Table 2 are then utilized within the framework of the SMT-based pivot translation by (1) translating the dialect input into the standard language using the SMT engines trained on the 20k data sets and (2) translating the standard language MT output into the foreign language using the SMT engines trained on the 160k data sets. The translation quality of the SMT-based pivot translation experiments are summarized in Table 3. Large gains of $6.2\%\sim25.4\%$ BLEU points compared to the direct translation results are obtained for all investigated language pairs, showing the effectiveness of pivot translation approaches for resource-limited language pairs. The largest gains are obtained for ja_{ku}, followed by ja_{os}, ja_{ky}, and ja_{ok}. Therefore, the easier the translation task, the larger the improvements of the pivot translation approach.

3.3 Bayesian Co-segmentation Model

The proposed method differs from the standard pivot translation approach in that a joint-source channel transducer trained from a Bayesian co-segmentation of the training corpus is used to transliterate the dialect input into the standard language, as described in Section 2.2. This process generates the co-segmented bilingual segments simultaneously in a monotone way, i.e., the order of consecutive segments on the source side as well as on the target side are the same. Similarly, the decoding process of the SMT approaches can also be carried out monotonically. In order to investigate the effect of word order differences for the given dialect to standard language transduction task, Table 4 compares the translation performance of SMT approaches with (*reorder-*

Table 4: Dialect to Standard Language Transduction

BLEU (%)

Engine	SRC (decoding)	ja_{ku}	ja_{ky} ($_{SRC \rightarrow ja}$)	ja_{ok}	ja_{os}
BCS	(monotone)	91.55	86.74	80.36	85.04
SMT	(monotone)	88.39	84.87	74.27	82.86
	(reordering)	88.39	84.73	74.26	82.66

ing) and without (*monotone*) distortion models to the monotone Bayesian co-segmentation approach (*BCS*). Only minor differences between SMT decoding with and without reordering are obtained. This shows that the grammatical structure of the dialect sentences and the standard language sentences are very similar, thus justifying the usage of monotone decoding strategies for the given task. The comparison of the SMT-based and the BCS-based transduction of the dialect sentences into the standard language shows that the Bayesian co-segmentation approach outperforms the SMT approach significantly, gaining 1.9% / 2.2% / 3.2% / 6.1% BLEU points for ja_{ky} / ja_{os} / ja_{ku} / ja_{ok}, respectively.

3.4 BCS-based Pivot Translation

The translation quality of the proposed method, i.e. the integration of the Bayesian co-segmentation models into the pivot translation framework, are given in Table 5. The overall gains of the proposed method compared to (a) the direct translation approach (see Table 2) and (b) the SMT-based pivot translation approach (see Table 3) are summarized in Table 6. The results show that the BCS-based pivot translation approach also largely outperforms the direct translation approach, gaining 5.9%~25.3% BLEU points. Comparing the two pivot translation approaches, the proposed BCS-based pivot translation method gains up to 0.8% BLEU points over the concatenation of SMT engines for the Indo-European target languages, but is not able to improve the translation quality for translating into Korean and Chinese. Interestingly, the SMT-based pivot translation approach seems to be better for language pairs where only small relative gains from the pivot translation approach are achieved when translating the dialect into a foreign language. For example, Korean is a language closely related to Japanese and the SMT models from the small data condition already seem to cover enough information to successfully translate the dialect languages into Korean. In the case of Chinese, the translation quality for even the large data condition SMT engines is relatively low. Therefore, improving the quality of the standard language input might have only a small impact on the overall pivot translation performance, if any at all. On the other hand, the proposed method can be successfully applied for the translation of language pairs where structural differences have a large impact on the translation quality. In such a translation task, the more accurate transduction of the dialect structure into the standard language can affect the overall translation performance positively.

Table 5: BCS-based Pivot Translation Quality

BLEU (%)

SRC / TRG	ja_{ku}	ja_{ky} ($BCS_{SRC \rightarrow ja}$+$SMT_{ja \rightarrow TRG}$)	ja_{ok}	ja_{os}
en	52.42	50.68	45.58	50.22
de	47.52	46.74	39.93	45.60
ru	45.29	44.08	38.39	43.53
hi	45.72	44.71	37.60	43.56
zh	45.15	43.92	40.15	44.06
ko	60.26	59.14	55.33	58.13

Table 6: Gains of BCS-based Pivot Translation

BLEU (%)

SRC / TRG	ja_{ku}	ja_{ky} (on SMT-based Pivot (Direct) Translation)	ja_{ok}	ja_{os}
en	+0.32 (+20.15)	+0.02 (+18.87)	+0.04 (+14.59)	+0.72 (+18.25)
de	+0.01 (+22.46)	+0.41 (+21.03)	+0.51 (+15.56)	+0.78 (+20.50)
ru	+0.70 (+22.17)	+0.25 (+20.89)	+0.14 (+16.09)	+0.66 (+21.46)
hi	-0.17 (+25.26)	+0.70 (+24.31)	+0.73 (+17.88)	+0.61 (+22.60)
zh	+0.01 (+12.43)	-0.34 (+10.77)	-0.81 (+7.49)	-0.14 (+11.10)
ko	-0.50 (+7.33)	-0.53 (+7.90)	-0.26 (+5.93)	-0.49 (+6.56)

4 Conclusion

In this paper, we proposed a new dialect translation method for resource-limited dialect languages within the framework of pivot translation. In the first step, a Bayesian co-segmentation model is learned to transduce character sequences in the dialect sentences into the word segmentation of the standard language. Next, an FST-based joint-source channel model is applied to unseen dialect input sentences to monotonically generate co-segmented bilingual segments from which the standard language segments are extracted. The obtained pivot sentence is then translated into the foreign language using a state-of-the-art phrase-based SMT engine trained on a large corpus.

Experiments were carried out for the translation of four Japanese dialects into four Indo-European as well as into two Asian languages. The results revealed that the Bayesian co-segmentation method largely improves the quality of the standard language sentence generated from a dialect input compared to SMT-based translation approaches. Although significant improvements of up to 0.8% in BLEU points are achieved for certain target languages, such as all of the investigated Indo-European languages, it is difficult to transfer the gains obtained by the Bayesian co-segmentation model to the outcomes for the pivot translation method.

Further research will have to investigate features like *language relatedness*, *structural differences*, and *translation model complexity* to identify indicators of translation quality that could enable the selection of BCS-based vs. SMT-based pivot translation approaches for specific language pairs to improve the overall system performance further.

In addition we would like to investigate the effects of using the proposed method for translating foreign languages into dialect languages. As the Bayesian co-segmentation model is symmetric with respect to source and target language, we plan to reuse the models learned for the experiments presented in this paper and hope to obtain new insights into the robustness of the Bayesian co-segmentation method when dealing with noisy data sets like machine translation outputs.

Acknowledgments

This work is partly supported by the Grant-in-Aid for Scientific Research (C) Number 19500137.

References

Cyril Allauzen, Michael Riley, Johan Schalkwyk, Wojciech Skut, and Mehryar Mohri. 2007. OpenFst: A General and Efficient Weighted Finite-State Transducer Library. In *Proc. of the 9th International Conference on Implementation and Application of Automata, (CIAA 2007)*, volume 4783 of *Lecture Notes in Computer Science*, pages 11–23. Springer. http://www.openfst.org.

Nicola Bertoldi, Madalina Barbaiani, Marcello Federico, and Roldano Cattoni. 2008. Phrase-Based statistical machine translation with Pivot Languages. In *Proc. of the 5th International Workshop on Spoken Language Translation (IWSLT)*, pages 143–149, Hawaii, USA.

Peter Brown, Stephen Della Pietra, Vincent Della Pietra, and Robert Mercer. 1993. The mathematics of statistical machine translation: Parameter estimation. *Computational Linguistics*, 19(2):263–311.

Ragul Chitturi and John Hansen. 2008. Dialect Classification for online podcasts fusing Acoustic and Language-based Structural and Semantic Information. In *Proc. of the 46th Annual Meeting of the Association for Computational Linguistics - Human Language Technologies (ACL-HLT), Companion Volume*, pages 21–24, Columbus, USA.

Adria de Gispert and Jose B. Marino. 2006. Catalan-English statistical machine translation without parallel corpus: bridging through Spanish. In *Proc. of 5th International Conference on Language Resources and Evaluation (LREC)*, pages 65–68, Genoa, Italy.

John DeNero, Alex Bouchard-Côté, and Dan Klein. 2008. Sampling Alignment Structure under a Bayesian Translation Model. In *Proc. of Conference on Empirical Methods on Natural Language Processing (EMNLP)*, Hawaii, USA.

Andrew Finch and Eiichiro Sumita. 2010. A Bayesian Model of Bilingual Segmentation for Transliteration. In *Proc. of the 7th International Workshop on Spoken Language Translation (IWSLT)*, pages 259–266, Paris, France.

Nizar Habash, Owen Rambow, and George Kiraz. 2005. Morphological Analysis and Generation for Arabic Dialects. In *Proc. of the ACL Workshop on Computational Approaches to Semitic Languages*, pages 17–24, Ann Arbor, USA.

Wilbert Heeringa, Peter Kleiweg, Charlotte Gosskens, and John Nerbonne. 2006. Evaluation of String Distance Algorithms for Dialectology. In *Proc. of the Workshop on Linguistic Distances*, pages 51–62, Sydney, Australia.

Sittichai Jiampojamarn, Kenneth Dwyer, Shane Bergsma, Aditya Bhargava, Qing Dou, Mi-Young Kim, and Grzegorz Kondrak. 2010. Transliteration Generation and Mining with Limited Training Resources. In *Proc. of the 2010 Named Entities Workshop (NEWS)*, pages 39–47, Uppsala, Sweden.

Genichiro Kikui, Seiichi Yamamoto, Toshiyuki Takezawa, and Eiichiro Sumita. 2006. Comparative study on corpora for speech translation. *IEEE Transactions on Audio, Speech and Language*, 14(5):1674–1682.

Philipp Koehn, Alexandra Birch, and Ralf Steinberger. 2009. 462 Machine Translation Systems for Europe. In *Proc. of the MT Summit XII*, Ottawa, Canada.

Chun-Jen Lee and Jason S. Chang. 2003. Acquisition of English-Chinese transliterated word pairs from parallel-aligned texts using a statistical machine transliteration model. In *Proc. of the HLT-NAACL 2003 Workshop on Building and using parallel texts, Volume 3*, pages 96–103, Edmonton, Canada.

Haizhou Li, Min Zhang, and Jian Su. 2004. A joint source-channel model for machine transliteration. In *Proc. of the 42nd ACL*, pages 159–166, Barcelona, Spain.

Daichi Mochihashi, Takeshi Yamada, and Naonori Ueda. 2009. Bayesian unsupervised word segmentation with nested Pitman-Yor language modeling. In *Proc of the Joint Conference of the 47th Annual Meeting of the ACL and the 4th International Joint Conference on Natural Language Processing of the AFNLP (ACL-IJCNLP)*, pages 100–108, Suntec, Singapore.

John Nerbonne and Wilbert Heeringa. 1997. Measuring Dialect Distance Phonetically. In *Proc. of the ACL Special Interest Group in Computational Phonology*, pages 11–18, Madrid, Spain.

Sara Noeman and Amgad Madkour. 2010. Language Independent Transliteration Mining System Using Finite State Automata Framework. In *Proc. of the 2010 Named Entities Workshop (NEWS)*, pages 57–61, Uppsala, Sweden.

Franz Josef Och and Hermann Ney. 2003. A Systematic Comparison of Various Statistical Alignment Models. *Computational Linguistics*, 29(1):19–51.

Kishore Papineni, Salim Roukos, Todd Ward, and Wei-Jing Zhu. 2002. BLEU: a method for automatic evaluation of machine translation. In *Proc. of the 40th Annual Meeting on Association for Computational Linguistics (ACL)*, pages 311–318, Philadelphia, USA.

Michael Paul, Hirofumi Yamamoto, Eiichiro Sumita, and Satoshi Nakamura. 2009. On the Importance of Pivot Language Selection for Statistical Machine Translation. In *Proc. of the North American Chapter of the Association for Computational Linguistics - Human Language Technologies (NAACL HLT)*, pages 221–224, Boulder, USA.

Michael Paul, Andrew Finch, and Eiichiro Sumita. 2011. Word Segmentation for Dialect Translation. *LNCS Lectures Note in Computer Science, Springer*, 6609:55–67.

Hassan Sawaf. 2010. Arabic Dialect Handling in Hybrid Machine Translation. In *Proc. of the 9th Conference of the Association for Machine Translation in the Americas (AMTA)*, Denver, USA.

Yves Scherrer. 2007. Adaptive String Distance Measures for Bilingual Dialect Lexicon Induction. In *Proc. of the ACL Student Research Workshop*, pages 55–60, Prague, Czech Republic.

Andreas Stolcke. 2002. SRILM - an extensible language modeling toolkit. In *Proc. of the International Conference on Spoken Language Processing (ICSLP), Volume 2*, pages 901–904, Denver, USA.

Keita Tsuji and Kyo Kageura. 2006. Automatic generation of JapaneseEnglish bilingual thesauri based on bilingual corpora. *J. Am. Soc. Inf. Sci. Technol.*, 57:891–906.

Masao Utiyama and Hitoshi Isahara. 2007. A Comparison of Pivot Methods for Phrase-Based Statistical Machine Translation. In *Proc. of Human Language Technologies (HLT)*, pages 484–491, New York, USA.

Hua Wu and Haifeng Wang. 2007. Pivot Language Approach for Phrase-Based Statistical Machine Translation. In *Proc. of the 45th Annual Meeting of the Association for Computational Linguistics (ACL)*, pages 856–863, Prague, Czech Republic.

Jia Xu, Jianfeng Gao, Kristina Toutanova, and Hermann Ney. 2008. Bayesian semi-supervised Chinese word segmentation for Statistical Machine Translation. In *Proc. of the 22nd International Conference on Computational Linguistics (COLING)*, pages 1017–1024, Manchester, United Kingdom.

Dialectal to Standard Arabic Paraphrasing to Improve Arabic-English Statistical Machine Translation

Wael Salloum and Nizar Habash
Center for Computational Learning Systems
Columbia University
{wael,habash}@ccls.columbia.edu

Abstract

This paper is about improving the quality of Arabic-English statistical machine translation (SMT) on dialectal Arabic text using morphological knowledge. We present a light-weight rule-based approach to producing Modern Standard Arabic (MSA) paraphrases of dialectal Arabic out-of-vocabulary (OOV) words and low frequency words. Our approach extends an existing MSA analyzer with a small number of morphological clitics, and uses transfer rules to generate paraphrase lattices that are input to a state-of-the-art phrase-based SMT system. This approach improves BLEU scores on a blind test set by 0.56 absolute BLEU (or 1.5% relative). A manual error analysis of translated dialectal words shows that our system produces correct translations in 74% of the time for OOVs and 60% of the time for low frequency words.

1 Introduction

Much work has been done on Modern Standard Arabic (MSA) natural language processing (NLP) and machine translation (MT). In comparison, research on dialectal Arabic (DA), the unstandardized spoken varieties of Arabic, is still lacking in NLP in general and MT in particular. In this paper we address the issue of MT out-of-vocabulary (OOV) terms and low frequency terms in highly dialectal Arabic text.

We present a light-weight rule-based approach to producing MSA morphological paraphrases of DA OOV words and low frequency words. However, we don't do lexical translation. Our approach extends an existing MSA analyzer to two DA varieties (Levantine and Egyptian) with less than 40 morphological clitics. We use 11 morphological transfer rules to generate paraphrase lattices that are input to a state-of-the-art phrase-based statistical MT (SMT) system. Our system improves BLEU scores on a blind test set by 0.56 absolute BLEU (or 1.5% relative). A manual error analysis of translated dialectal words shows that our system produces correct translations in 74% of the time for OOVs and 60% of the time for low frequency words.

The rest of this paper is structured as follows: Section 2 is related work, Section 3 presents linguistic challenges and motivation, Section 4 details our approach and Section 5 presents results evaluating our approach under a variety of conditions.

2 Related Work

Dialectal Arabic NLP Much work has been done in the context of MSA NLP (Habash, 2010). Specifically for Arabic-to-English SMT, the importance of tokenization using morphological analysis has been shown by many researchers (Lee, 2004; Zollmann et al., 2006; Habash and Sadat, 2006). In contrast, research on DA NLP is still in its early stages: (Kilany et al., 2002; Kirchhoff et al., 2003; Duh and Kirchhoff, 2005; Habash and Rambow, 2006; Chiang et al., 2006). Several researchers have explored the idea of exploiting existing MSA rich resources to build tools for DA NLP, e.g., Chiang et al. (2006) built syntactic parsers for DA trained on MSA treebanks. Such approaches typically expect the presence of tools/resources to relate DA words to their MSA variants or translations. Given that DA and MSA do not have much in terms of parallel corpora, rule-based methods to translate DA-to-MSA

Proceedings of EMNLP 2011, Conference on Empirical Methods in Natural Language Processing, pages 10–21,
Edinburgh, Scotland, UK, July 27–31, 2011.

or other methods to collect word-pair lists have been explored. For example, Abo Bakr et al. (2008) introduced a hybrid approach to transfer a sentence from Egyptian Arabic into MSA. This hybrid system consisted of a statistical system for tokenizing and tagging, and a rule-based system for constructing diacritized MSA sentences. Moreover, Al-Sabbagh and Girju (2010) described an approach of mining the web to build a DA-to-MSA lexicon. In the context of DA-to-English SMT, Riesa and Yarowsky (2006) presented a supervised algorithm for online morpheme segmentation on DA that cut the OOVs by half.

Machine Translation for Closely Related Languages Using closely related languages has been shown to improve MT quality when resources are limited. Hajič et al. (2000) argued that for very close languages, e.g., Czech and Slovak, it is possible to obtain a better translation quality by using simple methods such as morphological disambiguation, transfer-based MT and word-for-word MT. Zhang (1998) introduced a Cantonese-Mandarin MT that uses transformational grammar rules. In the context of Arabic dialect translation, Sawaf (2010) built a hybrid MT system that uses both statistical and rule-based approaches for DA-to-English MT. In his approach, DA is normalized into MSA using a dialectal morphological analyzer. This use of "resource-rich" related languages is a specific variant of the more general approach of using pivot/bridge languages (Utiyama and Isahara, 2007; Kumar et al., 2007). In the case of MSA and DA variants, it is plausible to consider the MSA variants of a DA phrase as monolingual paraphrases (Callison-Burch et al., 2006; Habash, 2008; Du et al., 2010).

This paper presents results on a rule-based system to generate alternative paraphrases for DA OOV words and low frequency words to help improve SMT from highly dialectal Arabic to English. Our work is most similar to Sawaf (2010)'s approach to DA *normalization* into MSA, although we shy away from the term in our work since we do not produce a single MSA version of the input to pass on to MSA-English MT. Instead we pass multiple paraphrases (or alternative normalizations) as a lattice to an SMT system, in a manner similar to Du et al. (2010). Certain aspects of our approach are similar to Riesa and Yarowsky (2006)'s, in that we use morphological analysis for DA to help DA-English MT; but unlike them and similar to Sawaf (2010), we use a rule-based approach to model DA morphology. Our morphological analysis implementation is quite similar to the approach taken by Abo Bakr et al. (2008), which extend existing MSA analyzers through rules; however, unlike them, we are not interested in generating MSA per se, but rather to use it as a bridge to English MT. Our interest in OOV words is similar to Habash (2008), who compared multiple techniques for handling MSA OOVs; however, unlike him, we target dialectal phenomena and we use lattices as input to the SMT system. Also related is the recent work by Nakov and Ng (2011), who use morphological knowledge to generate paraphrases for a morphologically rich language, Malay, to extend the phrase table in a Malay-to-English SMT system.

3 Challenge and Motivation

We are primarily interested in improving Arabic-English SMT on highly dialectal text. This particular type of text has many challenges. We discuss these challenges and motivate our research approach with an analysis of DA OOV terms in a state-of-the-art SMT system.

3.1 Arabic Linguistic Challenges

The Arabic language poses many challenges for NLP. Arabic is a morphologically complex language which includes rich inflectional morphology, expressed both templatically and affixationally, and several classes of attachable clitics. For example, the Arabic word وسيكتبونها *w+s+y-ktb-wn+hA*[1] 'and they will write it' has two proclitics (+و *w+* 'and' and +س *s+* 'will'), one prefix -ي *y-* '3rd person', one suffix ون- *-wn* 'masculine plural' and one pronominal enclitic ها+ *+hA* 'it/her'. Additionally, Arabic is written with optional diacritics that primarily specify short vowels and consonantal doubling. The absence of these diacritics together with the language's complex morphology lead to a high degree of ambiguity: the Buckwalter Arabic Morphological

[1]Arabic transliteration is presented in the Habash-Soudi-Buckwalter scheme (Habash et al., 2007): (in alphabetical order) *AbtθjHxdðrzsšSDTĎςγfqklmnhwy* and the additional symbols: ' ء, Â أ, Ǎ إ, Ā آ, ŵ ؤ, ŷ ئ, ħ ة, ý ى.

Analyzer (BAMA), for instance, produces an average of 12 analyses per word. Moreover, some letters in Arabic are often spelled inconsistently which leads to an increase in both sparsity (multiple forms of the same word) and ambiguity (same form corresponding to multiple words), e.g., variants of Hamzated Alif, أ Â or إ Ǎ, are often written without their Hamza (ء '): ا *A*; and the Alif-Maqsura (or dotless Ya) ى ý and the regular dotted Ya ي *y* are often used interchangeably in word final position (Kholy and Habash, 2010). Arabic complex morphology and ambiguity are handled using tools for disambiguation and tokenization (Habash and Rambow, 2005; Diab et al., 2007). For our SMT system, we preprocess the Arabic text so that it is tokenized in the Penn Arabic Treebank tokenization (Maamouri et al., 2004), Alif/Ya normalized and undiacritized. These measures have an important effect on reducing overall OOV rate (Habash, 2008).

3.2 Dialectal Arabic Challenges

Contemporary Arabic is in fact a collection of varieties: MSA, which has a standard orthography and is used in formal settings, and DAs, which are commonly used informally and with increasing presence on the web, but which do not have standard orthographies. There are several varieties of DA which primarily vary geographically, e.g., Levantine Arabic, Egyptian Arabic, etc. DAs differ from MSA phonologically, morphologically and to some lesser degree syntactically. The differences between MSA and DAs have often been compared to Latin and the Romance languages (Habash, 2006). The morphological differences are most noticeably expressed in the use of clitics and affixes that do not exist in MSA. For instance, the Levantine Arabic equivalent of the MSA example above is وحيكتبوها *w+H+y-ktb-w+hA* 'and they will write it'. The optionality of vocalic diacritics helps hide some of the differences resulting from vowel changes; compare the diacritized forms: Levantine *wHayuktubuwhA* and MSA *wasayaktubuwnahA*.

All of the NLP challenges of MSA described above are shared by DA. However, the lack of standard orthographies for the dialects and their numerous varieties pose new challenges. Additionally, DAs are rather impoverished in terms of available tools and resources compared to MSA; e.g., there is very little parallel DA-English corpora and almost no MSA-DA parallel corpora. The number and sophistication of morphological analysis and disambiguation tools in DA is very limited in comparison to MSA (Duh and Kirchhoff, 2005; Habash and Rambow, 2006; Abo Bakr et al., 2008). MSA tools cannot be effectively used to handle DA: Habash and Rambow (2006) report that less than two-thirds of Levantine verbs can be analyzed using an MSA morphological analyzer.

3.3 Dialectal Arabic OOVs

We analyzed the types of OOVs in our dev set against our large system (see Section 5) with an eye for dialectal morphology. The token OOV rate is 1.51% and the type OOV rate is 7.45%; although the token OOV rate may seem small, it corresponds to almost one third of all sentences having one OOV at least (31.48%). In comparison with MSA test sets, such as NIST MTEval 2006's token OOV rate of 0.8% (and 3.42% type OOV rate), these numbers are very high specially given the size of training data. Out of these OOVs, 25.9% have MSA readings or are proper nouns. The rest, 74.1%, are dialectal words. We classified the dialectal words into two types: words that have MSA-like stems and dialectal affixational morphology (affixes/clitics) and those that have dialectal stem and possibly dialectal morphology. The former set accounts for almost half of all OOVS (49.7%) or almost two thirds of all dialectal OOVS. In this paper we only target dialectal affixational morphology cases as they are the largest class involving dialectal phenomena that do not require extension to our stem lexica. The morphological coverage of the analyzer we use, ALMOR, which itself uses the BAMA databases is only 21% of all the OOV words. Our analyzer, ADAM, presented in Section 4.2, improves coverage substantially.

It is important to note that a word can be in-vocabulary (INV) but not have a correct possible translation in the phrase table. Some of these words may be of such low frequency that their various possible translations simply do not appear in the training data. Others may have a frequent MSA reading and an infrequent/unseen DA reading (or vice versa).

4 Approach

Our basic approach to address the issue of translational OOVs is to provide rule-based paraphrases of the source language words into words and phrases that are INV. The paraphrases are provided as alternatives in an input lattice to the SMT system. This particular implementation allows this approach to be easily integrated with a variety of SMT systems. The alternatives include different analyses of the same original word and/or translations into MSA. We focus on the question of Arabic dialects, although the approach can be extended to handle low frequency MSA words also that may have been mis-tokenized by the MSA preprocessing tools. As mentioned above, we only report in this work on dialect morphology translation to MSA and we leave lemma/word translation to future work. We identify four distinct operations necessary for this approach and evaluate different subsets of them in Section 5.

1. **Selection.** Identify the words to handle, e.g., OOVs or low frequency words.
2. **Analysis.** Produce a set of alternative analyses for each word.
3. **Transfer.** Map each analysis into one or more target analyses.
4. **Generation.** Generate properly tokenized forms of the target analyses.

The core steps of analysis-transfer-generation are similar to generic transfer-based MT (Dorr et al., 1999). In essence our approach can be thought of as a mini-rule-based system that is used to hybridize an SMT system (Simard et al., 2007; Sawaf, 2010).

4.1 Selection

The most obvious set of words to select for paraphrasing is the phrase-table OOV words. We identify them by comparing each word in the source text against all phrase-table singletons. Another set of words to consider includes low frequency words (DA or MSA), which are less likely to be associated with good phrase-table translations. We compute the frequency of such words against the original training data. We further extend the idea of frequency-based selection to typed-frequency selection in which we consider different frequency cut-offs for different types of words (MSA or DA). Evaluation and more details are presented in Section 5.3.

4.2 Analysis

Whereas much work has been done on MSA morphological analysis (Al-Sughaiyer and Al-Kharashi, 2004), a small handful of efforts have targeted the creation of dialectal morphology systems (Kilany et al., 2002; Habash and Rambow, 2006; Abo Bakr et al., 2008). In this section, we present a new dialectal morphological analyzer, ADAM, built as an extension to an already existing MSA analyzer. We only focus on extensions that address dialectal affixes and clitics, as opposed to stems, which we plan to address in future work. This approach to extending an MSA analyzer is similar to work done by Abo Bakr et al. (2008) and it contrasts as rather a shallow/quick-and-dirty solution compared to other more demanding efforts on building dialectal analyzers from scratch, such as the MAGEAD system (Habash and Rambow, 2006; Altantawy et al., 2011).

4.2.1 ADAM: Analyzer for Dialectal Arabic Morphology

ADAM is built on the top of BAMA database (Buckwalter, 2004) as used in the ALMOR morphological analyzer/generator (Habash, 2007), which is the rule-based component of the MADA system for morphological analysis and disambiguation of Arabic (Habash and Rambow, 2005; Roth et al., 2008). The ALMOR system presents analyses as lemma and feature-value pairs including clitics.

The BAMA databases contain three tables of Arabic stems, complex prefixes and complex suffixes[2] and three additional tables with constraints on matching them. MSA, according to the BAMA databases, has 1,208 complex prefixes and 940 complex suffixes, which correspond to 49 simple prefixes/proclitics and 177 simple suffixes/enclitics, respectively. The number of combinations in prefixes is a lot bigger than in suffixes, which explains the different proportions of complex affixes to simple affixes.

We extended the BAMA database through a

[2]We define a *complex prefix* as the full sequence of prefixes/proclitics that may appear at the beginning of a word. *Complex suffixes* are defined similarly.

Dialect Word	وماحيكتبلو *wmAHyktblw* ‘And he will not write for him’					
Analysis	Proclitics			[Lemma & Features]	Enclitics	
	w+	mA+	H+	yktb	+l	+w
	conj+	neg+	fut+	[katab IV subj:3MS voice:act]	+prep	$+pron_{3MS}$
	and+	not+	will+	he writes	+for	+him
Transfer	Word 1			Word 2	Word 3	
	Proclitics	[Lemma & Features]		[Lemma & Features]	[Lemma & Features]	Enclitic
	conj+	[lan]		[katab IV subj:3MS voice:act]	[li]	$+pron_{3MS}$
	and+	will not		he writes	for	+him
Generation	w+	ln		yktb	l	+h
MSA Phrase	ولن يكتب له *wln yktb lh* ‘And he will not write for him’					

Figure 1: An example illustrating the analysis-transfer-generation steps to translate a word with dialectal morphology into its MSA equivalent phrase.

set of rules that add new Levantine/Egyptian dialectal affixes and clitics by copying and extending existing MSA affixes/clitics. For instance, the dialectal future proclitic +ح *H+* ‘will’ has a similar behavior to the standard Arabic future particle +س *s+*. As such, an extension rule would create a copy of each occurrence of the MSA prefix and replace it with the dialectal prefix. The algorithm that uses this rule to extend the BAMA database adds the prefix `Ha/FUT_PART` and many other combinations involving it, e.g., `wa/PART+Ha/FUT_PART+ya/IV3MS`, and `fa/CONJ+Ha/FUT_PART+na/IV1P`. We reserve discussion of other more complex mappings with no exact MSA equivalence to a future publication on ADAM.

The rules (89 in total) introduce 11 new dialectal proclitics (plus spelling variants and combinations) and 27 dialectal enclitics (again, plus spelling variants and combinations). ADAM’s total of simple prefixes and suffixes increases to 60 (22% increase) and 204 (15% increase) over BAMA, respectively. The numbers for complex prefixes and suffixes increase at a faster rate to 3,234 (168% increase) and (142% increase), respectively.

As an example of ADAM output, consider the second set of rows in Figure 1, where a single analysis is shown.

4.2.2 ADAM **performance**

We conducted an analysis of ADAM’s behavior over the OOV set analyzed in Section 3.3. Whereas ALMOR (before ADAM) only produces analyzes for 21% of all the OOV words, ADAM covers almost 63%. Among words with dialectal morphology, ADAM’s coverage is 84.4%. The vast majority of the unhandled dialectal morphology cases involve a particular Levantine/Egyptian suffix +ش +š ‘not’. We plan to address these cases in the future. In about 10% of all the analyzed words, ADAM generates alternative dialectal readings to supplement existing ALMOR MSA analyses, e.g., بكتب *bktb* has an MSA (and coincidentally dialectal) analysis of ‘with books’ and ADAM also generates the dialectal only analysis ‘I write’.

4.3 Transfer

In the transfer step, we map ADAM’s dialectal analyses to MSA analyses. This step is implemented using a set of transfer rules (TR) that operate on the lemma and feature representation produced by ADAM. The TRs can change clitics, features or lemma, and even split up the dialectal word into multiple MSA word analyses. Crucially the input and output of this step are both in the lemma and feature representation (Habash, 2007). A particular analysis may trigger more than one rule resulting in multiple paraphrases. This only adds to the fan-out which started with the original dialectal word having multiple analyses.

Our current system uses 11 rules only, which were determined to handle all the dialectal clitics added in ADAM. As more clitics are added in ADAM, more TRs will be needed. As examples, two TRs which lead to the transfer output shown in the third set of rows in Figure 1 can be described as follows:[3]

[3]All of our rules are written in a declarative form, which

- *if the dialectal analysis shows future and negation proclitics, remove them from the word and create a new word, the MSA negative-future particle* لن *ln, to precede the current word and which inherits all proclitics preceding the future and negation proclitics.*
- *if the dialectal analysis shows the dialectal indirect object enclitic, remove it from the word and create a new word to follow the current word; the new word is the preposition* +ل *l+ with an enclitic pronoun that matches the features of the indirect object.*

In the current version evaluated in this paper, we always provide a lower-scored back-off analysis that removes all dialectal clitics as an option.

4.4 Generation

In this step, we generate Arabic words from all analyses produced by the previous steps. The generation is done using the general tokenizer TOKAN (Habash, 2007) to produce Arabic Treebank (ATB) scheme tokenizations. TOKAN is used in the baseline system to generate tokenizations for MSA from morphologically disambiguated input in the same ATB scheme (see Section 5.1). The various generated forms are added in the lattices, which are then input to the SMT system.

5 Evaluation on Machine Translation

5.1 Experimental Setup

We use the open-source Moses toolkit (Koehn et al., 2007) to build two phrase-based SMT systems trained on two different data conditions: a medium-scale MSA-only system trained using a newswire (MSA-English) parallel text with 12M words on the Arabic side (LDC2007E103) and a large-scale MSA/DA-mixed system (64M words on the Arabic side) trained using several LDC corpora including some limited DA data. Both systems use a standard phrase-based architecture. The parallel corpus is word-aligned using GIZA++ (Och and Ney, 2003). Phrase translations of up to 10 words are extracted in the Moses phrase table. The language model for both systems is trained on the English side of the large bitext augmented with English Gigaword data. We use a 5-gram language model with modified Kneser-Ney smoothing. Feature weights are tuned to maximize BLEU on the NIST MTEval 2006 test set using Minimum Error Rate Training (Och, 2003). This is only done on the baseline systems.

For all systems, the English data is tokenized using simple punctuation-based rules. The Arabic side is segmented according to the Arabic Treebank tokenization scheme (Maamouri et al., 2004) using the MADA+TOKAN morphological analyzer and tokenizer (Habash and Rambow, 2005) – v3.1 (Roth et al., 2008). The Arabic text is also Alif/Ya normalized (Habash, 2010). MADA-produced Arabic lemmas are used for word alignment.

Results are presented in terms of BLEU (Papineni et al., 2002), NIST (Doddington, 2002) and METEOR (Banerjee and Lavie, 2005) metrics.[4] However, all optimizations were done against the BLEU metric. All evaluation results are case insensitive.

All of the systems we present use the lattice input format to Moses (Dyer et al., 2008), including the baselines which do not need them. We do not report on the non-lattice baselines, but in initial experiments we conducted, they did not perform as well as the degenerate lattice version.

The Devtest Set Our devtest set consists of sentences containing at least one non-MSA segment (as annotated by LDC)[5] in the Dev10 audio development data under the DARPA GALE program. The data contains broadcast conversational (BC) segments (with three reference translations), and broadcast news (BN) segments (with only one reference, replicated three times). The data set contained a mix of Arabic dialects, with Levantine Arabic being the most common variety. The particular nature of the devtest being transcripts of audio data adds some challenges to MT systems trained on primarily written data in news genre. For instance, each of the source and references in the devtest set contained over 2,600 *uh*-like speech effect words (uh/ah/oh/eh), while the baseline translation system we used only generated 395. This led to severe

may be complicated to explain given the allotted space, as such we present only the functional description of the TRs.

[4]We use METEOR version 1.2 with four match modules: exact, stem, wordnet, and paraphrases.

[5]`http://www.ldc.upenn.edu/`

brevity penalty by the BLEU metric. As such, we removed all of these speech effect words in the source, references and our MT system output. Another similar issue was the overwhelming presence of commas in the English reference compared to the Arabic source: each reference had about 14,200 commas, while the source had only 64 commas. Our MT system baseline predicted commas in less than half of the reference cases. Similarly we remove commas from the source, references, and MT output. We do this to all the systems we compare in this paper. However, even with all of this preprocessing, the length penalty was around 0.95 on average in the large system and around 0.85 on average in the medium system. As such, we report additional BLEU sub-scores, namely the unigram and bigram precisions (Prec-1 and Prec-2, respectively), to provide additional understanding of the nature of our improvements.

We split this devtest set into two sets: a development set (dev) and a blind test set (test). We report all our analyses and experiments on the dev set and reserve the test set for best parameter runs at the end of this section. The splitting is done randomly at the document level. The dev set has 1,496 sentences with 32,047 untokenized Arabic words. The test set has 1,568 sentences with 32,492 untokenized Arabic words.

5.2 Handling Out-of-Vocabulary Words

In this section, we present our results on handling OOVs in our baseline MT system following the approach we described in Section 4. The results are summarized in Table 1. The table is broken into two parts corresponding to the large and medium systems. Each part contains results in BLEU, Prec-1 (unigram precision), Prec-2 (bigram precision), NIST and METEOR metrics. The performance of the large system is a lot better than the medium system in all experiments. Some of the difference is simply due to training size; however, another factor is that the medium system is trained on MSA only data while the large system has DA in its training data.

We compare the baseline system (first row) to two methods of OOV handling through dialectal paraphrase into MSA. The first method uses the ADAM morphological analyzer and generates directly skipping the transfer step to MSA. Although this may create implausible output for many cases, it is sufficient for some, especially through the system's natural addressing of orthographic variations. This method appears in Table 1 as ADAM Only. The second method includes the full approach as discussed in Section 4, i.e., including the transfer step.

The use of the morphological analyzer only method (ADAM Only) yields positive improvements across all metrics and training data size conditions. In the medium system, the improvement is around 0.42% absolute BLEU (or 2.1% relative). The large system improves by about 0.34% absolute BLEU (or almost 1% relative). Although these improvements are small, they are only accomplished by targeting a part of the OOV words (about 0.6% of all words).

The addition of transfer rules leads to further modest improvements in both large and medium systems according to BLEU; however, the NIST and METEOR metrics yield negative results in the medium system. A possible explanation for the difference in behavior is that paraphrase-based approaches to MT often suffer in smaller data conditions since the paraphrases they map into may themselves be OOVs against a limited system. Our transfer approach also has a tendency to generate longer paraphrases as options, which may have lead to more fragmentation in the METEOR score algorithm. In terms of BLEU scores, the full system (analysis and transfer) improves over the baseline on the order of 0.5% BLEU absolute. The relative BLEU score in the large and medium systems are 1.24% and 2.54% respectively.

All the systems in Table 1 do not drop unhandled OOVs, thus differing from the most common method of "handling" OOV, which is known to game popular MT evaluation metrics such as BLEU (Habash, 2008). In fact, if we drop OOVs in our baseline system, we get a higher BLEU score of 36.36 in the large system whose reported baseline gets 36.16 BLEU. That said, our best result with OOV handling produces a higher BLEU score (36.61) which is a nice result for doing the right thing and not just deleting problem words. All differences in BLEU scores in the large system are statistically significant above the 95% level. Statistical significance is computed using paired bootstrap resampling (Koehn, 2004).

	Large (64M words)					Medium (12M words)				
System	**BLEU**	**Prec-1**	**Prec-2**	**NIST**	**METEOR**	**BLEU**	**Prec-1**	**Prec-2**	**NIST**	**METEOR**
Baseline	36.16	74.56	45.04	8.9958	52.59	20.09	63.69	30.89	6.0039	40.85
ADAM **Only**	36.50	74.79	45.22	9.0655	52.95	20.51	64.37	31.22	**6.1994**	**41.80**
ADAM+**Transfer**	**36.61**	**74.85**	**45.37**	**9.0825**	**53.02**	**20.60**	**64.70**	**31.48**	6.1740	41.77

Table 1: Results for the dev set under large and medium training conditions. The baseline is compared to using dialectal morphological analysis only and analysis plus transfer to MSA. BLEU and METEOR scores are presented as percentages.

	Large (64M words)				
System	**BLEU**	**Prec-1**	**Prec-2**	**NIST**	**METEOR**
Baseline	36.16	74.56	45.04	8.9958	52.59
ADAM+**Transfer**	36.61	74.85	45.37	9.0825	53.02
+ **Freq** $x \leq 10$	36.71	74.89	45.50	9.0821	52.97
+ **Freq** $x_{MSA} \leq 10$	36.62	74.86	45.38	9.0816	52.96
+ **Freq** $x_{DIAMSA} \leq 13$	36.66	74.86	45.43	9.0836	53.01
+ **Freq** $x_{DIA} \leq 45$	36.73	**75.00**	45.57	**9.0961**	**53.03**
+ **Freq** $x_{MSA} \leq 10$ + $x_{DIAMSA} \leq 13$ + $x_{DIA} \leq 45$	**36.78**	74.96	**45.61**	9.0926	52.96

Table 2: Results for the dev set under large training condition, varying the set of words selected for MSA paraphrasing.

5.3 Extending Word Selection

Following the observation that some dialectal words may not pose a challenge to SMT since they appear frequently in training data, while some MSA words may be challenging since they are infrequent, we conduct a few experiments that widen the set of words selected for DA-MSA paraphrasing. We report our results on the large data condition only. Results are shown in Table 2. The baseline and best system from Table 1 are repeated for convenience.

We consider two types of word-selection extensions beyond OOVs. First, we consider frequency-based selection, where all words with less than or equal to a frequency of x are considered for paraphrasing in addition to being handled in the system's phrase table. Many low frequency words actually end up being OOVs as far as the phrase table is concerned since they are not aligned properly or at all by GIZA++. Secondly we consider a typed-frequency approach, where different frequency values are considered depending on wether a word is MSA only, dialect only or has both dialect and MSA readings. We determine MSA words to be those that have ALMOR analyses but no new ADAM analyses. Dialect-only words are those that have ADAM analyses but no ALMOR analyses. Finally, dialect/MSA words are those that have ALMOR analyses and get more dialect analyses through ADAM. The intuition behind the distinction is that problematic MSA only words may be much less frequent than problematic dialectal words.

We conducted a large number of experiments to empirically determine the best value for x in the frequency-based approach and x_{MSA}, x_{DIA}, and x_{DIAMSA} for the typed frequency approach. For the typed frequency approach, we took a greedy path to determine optimal values for each case and then used the best results collectively. Our best values are presented in Table 2. Both frequency-based approaches improve over the best results of only targeting OOVs. Further more, the fine-tuned typed frequency approach even yields further improvements leading to 0.62% absolute BLEU improvement over the baseline (or 1.71% relative). This score is statistically significant against the baseline and the ADAM+Transfer system as measured using paired bootstrap resampling (Koehn, 2004).

5.4 Blind Test Results

We apply our two basic system variants and best result with typed frequency selection to the blind test set. The results are shown in Table 3. The test set overall has slightly higher scores than the dev set, suggesting it may be easier to translate relatively.

	Large (64M words)				
System	**BLEU**	**Prec-1**	**Prec-2**	**NIST**	**METEOR**
Baseline	37.24	75.12	46.40	9.1599	52.93
ADAM **Only**	37.63	75.40	46.59	9.2414	53.39
ADAM**+Transfer**	37.71	75.46	46.70	9.2472	53.41
+ Freq $x_{MSA} \leq 10$ + $x_{DIAMSA} \leq 13$ + $x_{DIA} \leq 45$	**37.80**	**75.47**	**46.82**	**9.2578**	**53.44**

Table 3: Results for the blind test set under large training condition, comparing our best performing settings.

All of our system variants improve over the baseline and show the same rank in performance as on the dev set. Our best performer improves over the baseline by 0.56 absolute BLEU (or 1.5% relative). The relative increase in Prec-2 is higher than in Prec-1 suggesting perhaps that some improvements are coming from better word order.

5.5 Manual Error Analysis

We conduct two manual error analyses comparing the baseline to our best system. First we compare the baseline system to our best system applied only to OOVs. Among all 656 OOV tokens (1.51%) in our dev set we attempt to handle 417 tokens (0.96%) (i.e., 63.57% of possible OOVs) which could possibly affect 320 sentences (21.39%); however, we only see a change in 247 sentences (16.51%). We took a 50-sentence sample from these 247 sentences (our sample is 20%). We classified every occurrence of an OOV into not handled (the output has the OOV word), mistranslated (including deleted), or corrected (the output contains the correct translation); we focused on adequacy rather than fluency in this analysis. Table 4 presents some examples from the analysis set illustrating different behaviors. Among the OOVs in the sample (total 68 instances), 22% are not handled. Among the handled cases, we successfully translate 74% of the cases. Translation errors are mostly due to spelling errors, lexical ambiguity or proper names. There are no OOV deletions. This analysis suggests that our results reflect the correctness of the approach as opposed to random BLEU bias due to sentence length, etc.

In the second manual error analysis, we compare two systems to help us understand the effect of handling low frequency (LF) words: (a) our best system applied only to OOVs [OOV], and (b) our best system applied to OOVs and LF words [OOV+LF]. For LF words only (as compared to OOVs), we attempt to handle 669 tokens (1.54%) which could possibly affect 489 sentence (32.69%); however, we see a change in only 268 sentences (17.91%) (as compared to the OOV handling system). We took a 50-sentence sample from these sentences in the dev set where the output of the two systems is different (total 268 sentences; our sample is 19%). We classified each LF word into mistranslated or correct, and we annotated each case as dialectal, MSA, or tokenization error. Among the LF words in the sample (total 64 instances), the [OOV+LF] system successfully translated 55% of the cases while the [OOV] system successfully translated 50% of the cases. Overall, 11% of all LF words in our sample are due to a tokenization error, 34% are MSA, and 55% are dialectal. Among dialectal cases, the [OOV+LF] system successfully translated 60% of the cases while the [OOV] system successfully translated 42% of the cases. Among MSA cases, the [OOV+LF] system successfully translates 55% of the cases while the [OOV] system successfully translate 64% of the cases. The conclusion here is that (a) the majority of LF cases handled are dialectal and (b) the approach to handle them is helpful; however (c) the LF handling approach may hurt MSA words overall. Table 5 presents some examples from the analysis set illustrating different behaviors.

6 Conclusion and Future Work

We presented a light-weight rule-based approach to producing MSA paraphrases of dialectal Arabic OOV words and low frequency words. The generated paraphrase lattices result in improved BLEU scores on a blind test set by 0.56 absolute BLEU (or 1.5% relative). In the future, we plan to extend our system's coverage of phenomena in the handled dialects and on new dialects. We are interested in using ADAM to extend the usability of existing morphological disambiguation systems for MSA to the

Arabic	yςny ςn AlAzdHAmAt **btstxdmwn**[1] **AlbnšklAt**[2]?
Reference	You mean for traffic jams you **use**[1] **the bicycles**[2]?
Baseline	I mean, about the traffic **btstxdmwn**[1] **AlbnšklAt**[2]?
OOV-Handle	I mean, about the traffic **use**[1] **AlbnšklAt**[2]?
Arabic	nHnA **bntAml**[3] Anh fy hðA Almwqf tbdA msyr¯ħjdyd¯ħslmy¯ħmTlwb¯ħAlmnTq¯ħ
Reference	We **hope**[3] in this situation to start a new peace process that the region needs.
Baseline	We **bntAml**[3] that in this situation start a new march peaceful needed for the region.
OOV-Handle	We **hope**[3] that this situation will start a new march peaceful needed for the region.
Arabic	dktwr Anwr mAjd **ςšqy**[4] rŷys mrkz Alšrq AlAwsT lldrAsAt AlAstrAtyjy¯ħmn AlryAD ...
Reference	Dr. Anwar Majid **'Ishqi**[4] President of the Middle East Center for Strategic Studies from Riyadh ...
Baseline	Dr. anwar majed **ςšqy**[4] head of middle east center for strategic studies from riyadh ...
OOV-Handle	Dr. anwar majed **love**[4], president of the middle east center for strategic studies from riyadh ...

Table 4: Examples of different results of handling OOV words. Words of interest are bolded. Superscript indexes are used to link the related words within each example. Words with index 1 and 3 are correctly translated; the word with index 2 is not handled; and the word with index 4 is an incorrectly translated proper name.

Arabic	... wlðlk HtςAml mς Aljmyς ςly **hAlAsAs**.
Reference	... and I shall therefore deal with everyone on **this basis**.
OOV	... and therefore dealt with everyone **to think**.
OOV+LF	... and therefore dealt with everyone on **this basis**.
Arabic	... **tςydwn** nfs Alkrħ An lm ykn AswA ...
Reference	... **repeat** the same thing if not worse ...
OOV	... **to re -** the same if not worse ...
OOV+LF	... **bring back** the same if not worse ...

Table 5: Examples of different results of handling LF words. Words of interest are bolded. Both examples show a LF word mistranslated in the first system and successfully translated in the second system. The first examples shows a dialectal word while the second example shows an MSA word.

dialects, e.g., MADA. Furthermore, we want to automatically learn additional morphological system rules and transfer rules from limited available data (DA-MSA or DA-English) or at least use these resources to learn weights for the manually created rules.

Acknowledgments

This research was supported by the DARPA GALE program, contract HR0011-06-C-0022. Any opinions, findings, conclusions or recommendations expressed in this work are those of the authors and do not necessarily reflect the view of DARPA. We would like to thank Amit Abbi for help with the MT baseline. We also would like to thank John Makhoul, Richard Schwartz, Spyros Matsoukas, Rabih Zbib and Mike Kayser for helpful discussions and feedback and for providing us with the devtest data.

References

Hitham Abo Bakr, Khaled Shaalan, and Ibrahim Ziedan. 2008. A Hybrid Approach for Converting Written Egyptian Colloquial Dialect into Diacritized Arabic. In *The 6th International Conference on Informatics and Systems, INFOS2008*. Cairo University.

Rania Al-Sabbagh and Roxana Girju. 2010. Mining the Web for the Induction of a Dialectical Arabic Lexicon. In Nicoletta Calzolari, Khalid Choukri, Bente Maegaard, Joseph Mariani, Jan Odijk, Stelios Piperidis, Mike Rosner, and Daniel Tapias, editors, *LREC*. European Language Resources Association.

Imad A. Al-Sughaiyer and Ibrahim A. Al-Kharashi. 2004. Arabic morphological analysis techniques: A comprehensive survey. *Journal of the American Society for Information Science and Technology*, 55(3):189–213.

Mohamed Altantawy, Nizar Habash, and Owen Rambow. 2011. Fast Yet Rich Morphological Analysis. In *proceedings of the 9th International Workshop on Finite-State Methods and Natural Language Processing (FSMNLP 2011)*, Blois, France.

Satanjeev Banerjee and Alon Lavie. 2005. METEOR: An Automatic Metric for MT Evaluation with Improved Correlation with Human Judgments. In *Proceedings of the ACL Workshop on Intrinsic and Extrinsic Evaluation Measures for Machine Translation and/or Summarization*, pages 65–72, Ann Arbor, Michigan.

Tim Buckwalter. 2004. Buckwalter Arabic Morphological Analyzer Version 2.0. Linguistic Data Consortium, University of Pennsylvania. LDC Catalog No.: LDC2004L02, ISBN 1-58563-324-0.

Chris Callison-Burch, Philipp Koehn, and Miles Osborne. 2006. Improved statistical machine translation using paraphrases. In *Proceedings of the Human Language Technology Conference of the NAACL, Main Conference*, pages 17–24.

David Chiang, Mona Diab, Nizar Habash, Owen Rambow, and Safiullah Shareef. 2006. Parsing Arabic Dialects. In *Proceedings of the European Chapter of ACL (EACL)*.

Mona Diab, Kadri Hacioglu, and Daniel Jurafsky, 2007. *Arabic Computational Morphology: Knowledge-based and Empirical Methods*, chapter Automated Methods for Processing Arabic Text: From Tokenization to Base Phrase Chunking. Springer.

George Doddington. 2002. Automatic evaluation of machine translation quality using n-gram co-occurrence statistics. In *Human Language Technology*, pages 128–132, San Diego.

Bonnie J. Dorr, Pamela W. Jordan, and John W. Benoit. 1999. A Survey of Current Research in Machine Translation. In M. Zelkowitz, editor, *Advances in Computers, Vol. 49*, pages 1–68. Academic Press, London.

Jinhua Du, Jie Jiang, and Andy Way. 2010. Facilitating translation using source language paraphrase lattices. In *Proceedings of the 2010 Conference on Empirical Methods in Natural Language Processing*, EMNLP'10, pages 420–429, Cambridge, Massachusetts.

Kevin Duh and Katrin Kirchhoff. 2005. POS tagging of dialectal Arabic: a minimally supervised approach. In *Proceedings of the ACL Workshop on Computational Approaches to Semitic Languages*, Semitic '05, pages 55–62, Ann Arbor, Michigan.

Christopher Dyer, Smaranda Muresan, and Philip Resnik. 2008. Generalizing word lattice translation. In *Proceedings of ACL-08: HLT*, Columbus, Ohio.

Nizar Habash and Owen Rambow. 2005. Arabic Tokenization, Part-of-Speech Tagging and Morphological Disambiguation in One Fell Swoop. In *Proceedings of the 43rd Annual Meeting of the Association for Computational Linguistics (ACL'05)*, pages 573–580, Ann Arbor, Michigan.

Nizar Habash and Owen Rambow. 2006. MAGEAD: A Morphological Analyzer and Generator for the Arabic Dialects. In *Proceedings of the 21st International Conference on Computational Linguistics and 44th Annual Meeting of the Association for Computational Linguistics*, pages 681–688, Sydney, Australia.

Nizar Habash and Fatiha Sadat. 2006. Arabic Preprocessing Schemes for Statistical Machine Translation. In *Proceedings of the Human Language Technology Conference of the NAACL, Companion Volume: Short Papers*, pages 49–52, New York City, USA.

Nizar Habash, Abdelhadi Soudi, and Tim Buckwalter. 2007. On Arabic Transliteration. In A. van den Bosch and A. Soudi, editors, *Arabic Computational Morphology: Knowledge-based and Empirical Methods*. Springer.

Nizar Habash. 2006. On Arabic and its Dialects. *Multilingual Magazine*, 17(81).

Nizar Habash. 2007. Arabic Morphological Representations for Machine Translation. In A. van den Bosch and A. Soudi, editors, *Arabic Computational Morphology: Knowledge-based and Empirical Methods*. Springer.

Nizar Habash. 2008. Four Techniques for Online Handling of Out-of-Vocabulary Words in Arabic-English Statistical Machine Translation. In *Proceedings of ACL-08: HLT, Short Papers*, pages 57–60, Columbus, Ohio.

Nizar Habash. 2010. *Introduction to Arabic Natural Language Processing*. Morgan & Claypool Publishers.

Jan Hajič, Jan Hric, and Vladislav Kubon. 2000. Machine Translation of Very Close Languages. In *Proceedings of the 6th Applied Natural Language Processing Conference (ANLP'2000)*, pages 7–12, Seattle.

Ahmed El Kholy and Nizar Habash. 2010. Techniques for Arabic Morphological Detokenization and Orthographic Denormalization. In *Workshop on Language Resources and Human Language Technology for Semitic Languages in the Language Resources and Evaluation Conference (LREC)*, Valletta, Malta.

H. Kilany, H. Gadalla, H. Arram, A. Yacoub, A. El-Habashi, and C. McLemore. 2002. Egyptian Colloquial Arabic Lexicon. LDC catalog number LDC99L22.

Katrin Kirchhoff, Jeff Bilmes, Sourin Das, Nicolae Duta, Melissa Egan, Gang Ji, Feng He, John Henderson, Daben Liu, Mohamed Noamany, Pat Schone, Richard Schwartz, and Dimitra Vergyri. 2003. Novel Approaches to Arabic Speech Recognition: Report from the 2002 Johns Hopkins Summer Workshop. In *IEEE International Conference on Acoustics, Speech, and Signal Processing*, Hong Kong, China.

P. Koehn, H. Hoang, A. Birch, C. Callison-Burch, M. Federico, N. Bertoldi, B. Cowan, W. Shen, C. Moran, R. Zens, C. Dyer, O. Bojar, A. Constantin, and E. Herbst. 2007. Moses: open source toolkit for statistical machine translation. In *Proceedings of the 45th Annual Meeting of the Association for Computational Linguistics Companion Volume Proceedings of the Demo and Poster Sessions*, pages 177–180, Prague, Czech Republic.

Philipp Koehn. 2004. Statistical significance tests formachine translation evaluation. In *Proceedings of the Empirical Methods in Natural Language Processing Conference (EMNLP'04)*, Barcelona, Spain.

Shankar Kumar, Franz J. Och, and Wolfgang Macherey. 2007. Improving word alignment with bridge languages. In *Proceedings of the 2007 Joint Conference on Empirical Methods in Natural Language Processing and Computational Natural Language Learning (EMNLP-CoNLL)*, pages 42–50, Prague, Czech Republic.

Young-Suk Lee. 2004. Morphological Analysis for Statistical Machine Translation. In *Proceedings of the 5th Meeting of the North American Chapter of the Association for Computational Linguistics/Human Language Technologies Conference (HLT-NAACL04)*, pages 57–60, Boston, MA.

Mohamed Maamouri, Ann Bies, Tim Buckwalter, and Wigdan Mekki. 2004. The Penn Arabic Treebank: Building a Large-Scale Annotated Arabic Corpus. In *NEMLAR Conference on Arabic Language Resources and Tools*, pages 102–109, Cairo, Egypt.

Preslav Nakov and Hwee Tou Ng. 2011. Translating from Morphologically Complex Languages: A Paraphrase-Based Approach. In *Proceedings of the Meeting of the Association for Computational Linguistics (ACL'2011)*, Portland, Oregon, USA.

F. J. Och and H. Ney. 2003. A systematic comparison of various statistical alignment models. *Computational Linguistics*, 29(1):19–51.

Franz Josef Och. 2003. Minimum Error Rate Training for Statistical Machine Translation. In *Proceedings of the 41st Annual Conference of the Association for Computational Linguistics*, pages 160–167, Sapporo, Japan.

Kishore Papineni, Salim Roukos, Todd Ward, and Wei-Jing Zhu. 2002. BLEU: a Method for Automatic Evaluation of Machine Translation. In *Proceedings of the 40th Annual Meeting of the Association for Computational Linguistics*, pages 311–318, Philadelphia, PA.

Jason Riesa and David Yarowsky. 2006. Minimally Supervised Morphological Segmentation with Applications to Machine Translation. In *Proceedings of the 7th Conference of the Association for Machine Translation in the Americas (AMTA06)*, pages 185–192, Cambridge,MA.

Ryan Roth, Owen Rambow, Nizar Habash, Mona Diab, and Cynthia Rudin. 2008. Arabic Morphological Tagging, Diacritization, and Lemmatization Using Lexeme Models and Feature Ranking. In *Proceedings of ACL-08: HLT, Short Papers*, pages 117–120, Columbus, Ohio.

Hassan Sawaf. 2010. Arabic dialect handling in hybrid machine translation. In *Proceedings of the Conference of the Association for Machine Translation in the Americas (AMTA)*, Denver, Colorado.

Michel Simard, Nicola Ueffing, Pierre Isabelle, and Roland Kuhn. 2007. Rule-based translation with statistical phrase-based post-editing. In *Proceedings of the Second Workshop on Statistical Machine Translation*, pages 203–206, Prague, Czech Republic.

Masao Utiyama and Hitoshi Isahara. 2007. A comparison of pivot methods for phrase-based statistical machine translation. In *HLT-NAACL*, pages 484–491.

Xiaoheng Zhang. 1998. Dialect MT: a case study between Cantonese and Mandarin. In *Proceedings of the 36th Annual Meeting of the Association for Computational Linguistics and 17th International Conference on Computational Linguistics*, ACL '98, pages 1460–1464, Montreal, Canada.

Andreas Zollmann, Ashish Venugopal, and Stephan Vogel. 2006. Bridging the Inflection Morphology Gap for Arabic Statistical Machine Translation. In *Proceedings of the Human Language Technology Conference of the NAACL, Companion Volume: Short Papers*, pages 201–204, New York City, USA.

PaddyWaC: A Minimally-Supervised Web-Corpus of Hiberno-English

Brian Murphy
Centre for Mind/Brain Sciences,
University of Trento
38068 Rovereto (TN), Italy
brian.murphy@unitn.it

Egon Stemle
Centre for Mind/Brain Sciences,
University of Trento
38068 Rovereto (TN), Italy
egon.stemle@unitn.it

Abstract

Small, manually assembled corpora may be available for less dominant languages and dialects, but producing web-scale resources remains a challenge. Even when considerable quantities of text are present on the web, finding this text, and distinguishing it from related languages in the same region can be difficult. For example less dominant variants of English (e.g. New Zealander, Singaporean, Canadian, Irish, South African) may be found under their respective national domains, but will be partially mixed with Englishes of the British and US varieties, perhaps through syndication of journalism, or the local reuse of text by multinational companies. Less formal dialectal usage may be scattered more widely over the internet through mechanisms such as wiki or blog authoring. Here we automatically construct a corpus of Hiberno-English (English as spoken in Ireland) using a variety of methods: filtering by national domain, filtering by orthographic conventions, and bootstrapping from a set of Ireland-specific terms (slang, place names, organisations). We evaluate the national specificity of the resulting corpora by measuring the incidence of topical terms, and several grammatical constructions that are particular to Hiberno-English. The results show that domain filtering is very effective for isolating text that is topic-specific, and orthographic classification can exclude some non-Irish texts, but that selected seeds are necessary to extract considerable quantities of more informal, dialectal text.

1 Introduction

For less dominant language variants, corpora are usually painstakingly constructed by hand. This results in high quality collections of text, classified and balanced by genre, register and modality. But the process is time-consuming and expensive, and results in relatively small resources. For example the International Corpus of English (ICE) project (Greenbaum, 1996) has already resulted in the publication of corpora covering ten dialects of English, following a common schema, but the individual corpora are limited to approximately one million words.

An alternative is to use automatic methods to harvest corpora from the Web. Identification of major languages is a robust technology, and where the regional boundaries of a language or dialect correspond closely to a national top-level internet domain, very large collections (of several billion words) can now can be produced easily, with close to no manual intervention (Baroni et al., 2009). These methods can also deal with some issues of text quality found on the web, successfully extracting coherent pieces of running text from web pages (i.e. discarding menu text, generic headings, copyright and other legal notices), reducing textual duplication, and identifying spam, portal pages and other files that do not contain linguistically interesting text.

Corpora of minor languages that lack their own domain, but that have clear orthographic differences from more dominant neighbouring languages can be collected automatically by using a small set of seed documents, from which language-specific search terms can be extracted (Scannell, 2007). These methods, combined with automated language identification methods, can quickly produce large, clean collections with close to no manual intervention.

However for language variants that do not have their own domain (e.g. Scots, Bavarian), it is less clear that such web corpora can be automatically constructed. Smaller or politically less dominant countries that do have their own domain (e.g. Belgium, New Zealand), may also find the language of their "national" web strongly influenced by other language varieties, for example through syndication of journalistic articles, or materials published by foreign companies.

In this paper we use minimally supervised methods (Baroni and Bernardini, 2004; Baroni et al., 2009) to quickly and cheaply build corpora of Hiberno-English (English as spoken in Ireland), which are many times larger than ICE-Ireland, the largest published collection

Proceedings of EMNLP 2011, Conference on Empirical Methods in Natural Language Processing, pages 22–29,
Edinburgh, Scotland, UK, July 27–31, 2011.

currently available (Kallen and Kirk, 2007). We investigate several combinations of strategies (based on domain names, and on regional variations in vocabulary and orthography) to distinguish text written in this minor language variant from related dominant variants (US and UK English). We validate the specificity of the resulting corpora by measuring the incidence of Ireland-specific language, both topically (the frequency with which Irish regions and organisations are mentioned), and structurally, by the presence of grammatical constructions that are particular to Hiberno-English. We also compare our corpus to another web-corpus of Hiberno-English that is in development (*Crúbadán*, Scannell, personal communication) that relies on domain filtering of crawled web-pages.

The results show that filtering by national domain is very effective in identifying text that deals with Irish topics, but that the grammar of the resulting text is largely standard. Using a set of seed terms tailored to the language variant (Irish slang, names of Ireland-based organisations, loanwords from Irish Gaelic), yields text which is much more particular to Hiberno-English usage. At the same time, such tailored seed terms increase the danger of finding "non-authentic" uses of Irishisms (sometimes termed *paddywhackery* or *oirish*), either in fictional dialogues, or in documents discussing distinctive patterns in Irish English. The application of a British/American spelling filter has less clear effects, increasing topical incidence slightly, while reducing structural incidences somewhat.

The paper proceeds as follows: in the next section we introduce Hiberno-English, situating it relative to other variants of English, and concentrating on the characteristic features that will be used as metrics of "Irishness" of text retrieved from the Web. Next we describe the process by which several candidate corpora of Hiberno-English were constructed (section 3), and the methods we used to quantify incidence of distinctive usage (section 4). In the final two sections we compare the incidence of these markers with those found in corpora of other variants of English (UK, US), Scannell's IE-domain filtered corpus, and a hand-crafted corpus of Hiberno-English (ICE-Ireland), and reflect on the wider applicability of these methods to variants of other languages and orthographies.

2 Structures and Lexicon of Hiberno-English

Hiberno-English differs in a range of ways from other varieties of English. In broad terms it can be grouped with British English, in that its lexicon, grammar and orthographic conventions are more similar to that of Great Britain, than to that of North America. For example with lexical variants such as *bumper/fender, rubbish bin/trash can, lift/elevator* and *zed/zee* it shares the former British usage rather than the latter American usage, though there are exceptions (in Irish usage the North Americans term *truck* is replacing the British *lorry*). Similarly in syntax it tends to follow British conventions, for instance *He's familiar with X* rather than *X is familiar to him*, *write to me* rather than *write me* and the acceptability of singular verbal marking with group subjects, as in *the team are pleased* – though there are counterexamples again, in that Irish English tends to follow American dialects in dispensing with the *shall/will* distinction. Most obviously, Irish writing uses British spellings rather than American spellings.

However, there are still dialectal differences between Irish and British English. Beyond the usual regional differences that one might find between the words used in different parts of England, the English spoken in Ireland is particularly influenced by the Irish language (Gaelic, *Gaeilge*) (Kirk and Kallen, 2007). While English is the first language of the overwhelming majority of residents of Ireland (estimates of Irish mother-tongue speakers are of the order of 50,000, or about 1% of the population), Irish retains status as the first official language of the Republic of Ireland, maintained as a core subject at all levels of school education, and through state-maintained radio and television channels. As recently as the early 19th century, Irish was the majority language, and so many traces of it remain in modern Hiberno-English, in the form of Irish loan-words (e.g. *slán* 'goodbye', *gaelscoil* 'Irish (speaking) school'), Anglicizations (e.g. 'gansey', jumper, from Irish *geansaí*), and composites (e.g. 'jackeen', a pejorative term for Dubliners, combining the Irish diminutive *-ín* with the English 'Jack').

In this paper we take a series of characteristic terms and structures from Hiberno-English, mostly inspired by (Kirk and Kallen, 2007), and use them as markers of the Irishness of the text we assemble from the web. While there are many more interesting grammatical differences between Hiberno-English and other variants (e.g. perfective use of the simple present: *I know that family for years*), we restrict ourselves to those that can be automatically identified in a corpus through searching of plain text, or of shallow syntactic patterns (parts of speech).

The first marker we use is to measure the incidence of a set of terms that are topically related to Ireland: proper names of Ireland-based organisations, and geographical terms. The method for assembling this list is described in section 4.

The most simple structure that we use as a marker of Hiberno-English is the contraction *I amn't* (*I'm not* or *I ain't* in other varieties). The next is the "after" perfective, which often expresses immediacy, and a negative outcome:

(1) I'm after losing my wallet
'I just lost my wallet'

A further structure that is novel from the point of view of other variants of English is a particular use of verbs that take a complement that expresses a question (most commonly *ask, wonder, see* and *know*), without the use of a complementizer such as *if* or *whether* and with an inversion of subject-verb order (typical of interrogatives):

(2) I wonder is he coming"
'I wonder if/whether he is coming'

Finally we consider the expanded usage of reflexive pronouns in Hiberno-English, where they may be used for emphasis, in any argument position, and without being anaphorically bound, as is usually required. Here we limit ourselves to subject position reflexives, which can be identified from word order patterns, without any deeper semantic analysis:

(3) himself is in big trouble
'he is in big trouble'

With the exception of the *amn't* contraction, all of these phenomena are demonstrated by (Kirk and Kallen, 2007) to be common in the ICE-Ireland corpus, though somewhat less common in Northern Irish portion of that collection, and to be very rare or completely absent in the ICE-GB corpus of the English of Britain (Nelson et al., 2002). Significantly, these constructions are found predominantly in the spoken language portion of the ICE-Ireland corpus, suggesting that speakers are perhaps aware that they are not "standard" English, and so not considered appropriate in the written register.

3 Constructing a Web-Corpus of Hiberno-English

Within the WaCky initiative (Web-as-Corpus kool ynitiative) (Baroni and Bernardini, 2006) a community of linguists and information technology specialists developed a set of tools to selectively crawl sections of the Web, and then process, index and search the resulting data. Contributions like BootCaT (Baroni and Bernardini, 2004), an iterative procedure to bootstrap specialised corpora and terms from the Web, have been successfully used in a range of projects: first in the construction of the *WaCky corpora*, a collection of very large (>1 billion words) corpora of English (ukWaC), German (deWaC) and Italian (itWaC); and subsequently by other groups, e.g. noWaC and jpWaC (Baroni et al., 2009; Guevara, 2010; Erjavec et al., 2008).

Here we use BootCaT to build seven prototype corpora of Hiberno-English, and evaluate the dialect-specificity of each by measuring the incidence of proper terms and constructions that are associated with this language variant. Additionally, we use ukWaC as the de-facto standard British English Web corpus, and construct a medium size web-corpus of the US domain to represent American usage. Each corpus is preprocessed and formatted for the IMS Open Corpus Workbench (CWB, (Christ, 1994; Web, 2008)), a generic query engine for large text corpora that was developed for applications in computational lexicography.

BootCaT first takes a set of manually assembled seed terms, these (possibly multi-word) terms are randomly combined, and then are used as search queries with a Web search engine; the HTML documents of the top results are downloaded and cleaned to extract running text and discard all web-markup. Preprocessing and formatting for the CWB consists of tokenising, lemmatising, and part-of-speech tagging the corpus, and then converting the result into CWB's internal format; we replicated the processing stages employed for ukWaC.

The construction of the nine corpora differs on three dimensions:

Seeds: two seed sets were used namely, an Hiberno-English one (IEs), and the original ukWaC list of mid-frequency terms (UKs) from the British National Corpus (Burnard, 1995); the Irish seeds were used in pairs and triples to attempt to vary the degree of regional specificity.

TLDs: two types of top-level internet domain (TLD) restrictions were imposed during (or after) the construction of the corpora; either no restriction was imposed (.ALL), or a corpus was filtered by a specific national TLD (e.g. .ie).

Spelling: two types of spelling filter were imposed; either none, or an 'orthographic convention factor' (OCF) was calculated to detect American and British spellings, and a corpus was filtered accordingly (BrEn).

The IE seeds contained 81 seed terms, gathered using one author's native intuition, and words indicated as being specific to Irish English by the Oxford English Dictionary, and from various Web pages about Hiberno-English. 76 single-word and 5 two-word terms were used falling into three main categories: Irish place names, regional variant terms (mostly slang), and load words from Irish Gaelic (many being state institutions). The full listing of terms is given here:

Place names: Dublin, Galway, Waterford, Drogheda, Antrim, Derry, Kildare, Meath, Donegal, Armagh, Wexford, Wicklow, Louth, Kilkenny, Westmeath, Offaly, Laois, Belfast, Cavan, Sligo, Roscommon, Monaghan, Fermanagh, Carlow, Longford, Leitrim, Navan, Ennis, Tralee, Leinster, Connaught, Munster, Ulster

Regional variants: banjaxed (wrecked), craic (fun), fecking (variant of fucking), yoke (thing), yer man/one/wan (that man/woman), culchie (country dweller), da (father), footpath (pavement), gaff (home), gobshite (curse), gurrier (young child), jackeen (Dubliner), jacks (toilet), janey mac (exclamation), jaysus (variant of exclamation "jesus"), kip (sleep; hovel), knacker (Traveller, gypsy), knackered (wrecked), langer (penis; idiot), langers/langered (drunk), scallion (spring onion), skanger (disgusting person), strand (beach, seaside), scuttered (drunk), boreen (small road), gob (mouth; spit), eejit (variant of idiot), lough (lake), fooster (dawdle), barmbrack (traditional Hallow'een cake), shebeen (unlicensed bar), bogman (contry dweller), old one (old lady), quare (variant queer), gansey (pullover)

Loan words: garda, gardaí (police), taoiseach (prime minister), dáil (parliament), Sláinte ("cheers"), Gaeltacht (Irish speaking areas), Seanad (senate), Tánaiste (deputy prime minister), ceol ((traditional Irish) music), slán ("goodbye"), grá (affection, love for), gaelscoil (Irish speaking school)

These seed terms were combined into a set of 3000 3-tuple (3T) and a set of 3000 2-tuple (2T) search queries, i.e. two-word terms were enclosed in inverted commas to form one single term for the search engine. For 3T this resulted in over 80% 3-tuples with 3 single-word terms, and slightly over 17% with 2 single-word terms, and the remaining percentages for 3-tuples with 1 single-word and no single-word terms; for 2T this resulted in almost 88% 2-tuples with 2 single-word terms, almost 12% with only 1 single-word terms, and less than 1% with no single-word terms. The UK seeds were the original ones used during the construction of the ukWaC corpus and they were combined into 3000 3-tuple search queries.

No TLD restriction means that the search engine was not instructed to return search results within a specific domain, and hence, documents originate from typical English-language domains (.com, .ie, .uk, etc.) but also from .de and potentially any other. A restriction meant that the documents could only originate from one TLD.

No spelling filter means that nothing was done. The OCF indicates the degree to which terms within a document are predominantly spelled according to one predefined word list relative to another. The number of term intersections with each list is counted and OCF is calculated as the difference between counts over their sum. To simplify matters, we utilised a spell-checker to return the list of known words from a document, this corresponds to checking a document for spelling errors and only keeping the non-erroneous words. In our case we used an en_GB dictionary, an en_US one, and the two together. The three lists yield the needed numbers of words only known by one of the two dictionaries, and, hence unknown by the other dictionary, and the ratio in the range of $[-1, +1]$ can be calculated.

The search engine we used for all queries was Yahoo (Yahoo! Inc., 1995); for all search queries English results were requested, that is we relied on the search engine's built-in language identification algorithm[1], and from all search queries the top 10 results were used. Cleaning of the Web pages (termed *boilerplate removal*) was accomplished by BootCaT's implementation of the BTE method (Finn et al., 2001); it strives to extract the main body of a Web page, that is the largest contiguous text area with the least amount of intervening non-text elements (HTML tags), and discards the rest.

Several corpora were constructed from the Irish seeds using 2- or 3-tuple search terms: either without restricting the TLDs; subsequent restriction to the .ie TLD; or subsequent filtering according to spelling. Corpora were also constructed with the search engine instructed to directly return documents from the .us or the .ie TLD, respectively, where the latter one was later also filtered according to spelling. The ukWaC corpus is restricted to the .uk TLD.

4 Evaluating Variety Specificity of the Corpus

To evaluate the dialectal specificity of the text in each putative corpus of Hiberno-English, we measured the incidence of several characteristic terms and structures. The same phenomena were counted in corpora of US and UK English (identified as that found under the .us and .uk TLDs respectively) to establish baseline frequencies. All corpora were HTML-cleaned, lemmatised and part-of-speech tagged using the same methods described above, and searches were made with identical, case-insensitive, queries in the CQP language.

First we quantified topical specificity by searching for a set of Irish geographical terms (towns, counties, regions), and Ireland-based organisations (companies, NGOs, public-private bodies), to identify text which is "about Ireland". There were 80 terms, evenly split between the two categories. In this list we avoided proper names which are orthographically identical to content words (e.g. Down, Cork, Clones, Trim, Limerick, Mallow, Mayo), given names (Clare, Kerry, Tyrone), place names found in other territories (Baltimore, Skibbereen, Newbridge, Westport, Passage West), or names that might be found as common noun-phrases (e.g. Horse Racing Ireland, Prize Bond Company, Electricity Supply Board). While political terms might have been appropriate markers (e.g. the political party Fianna Fáil; the parliamentary speaker the Ceann Comhairle), the seed terms we used contained many governmental institutions, and so this could be considered an unfairly biased diagnostic marker. The full list of terms is given below.

Topical terms: ActionAid, Aer, Aer, Allied, An, Arklow, Athlone, Athy, Balbriggan, Ballina, Ballinasloe, Bantry, Bord, Bord, Bord, Buncrana, Bundoran, Bus, Carrick-on-Suir, Carrickmacross, Cashel, Castlebar, Christian, Clonakilty, Clonmel, Cobh, Coillte, Comhl(ála)mh, Connacht, C(ólo)ras, Donegal, Dublin, Dublin, Dungarvan, Eircom, EirGrid, Enniscorthy, Fermoy, Fyffes, Glan-

[1] This restriction is very effective at distinguishing non-English from English content, but returns content from any English variant.

bia, Gorta, Grafton, Greencore, Iarnr(ólo)d, IONA, Irish, Irish, Irish, Kerry, Kilkee, Kilrush, Kinsale, Laois, Leixlip, Letterkenny, Listowel, Listowel, Loughrea, Macroom, Mullingar, Naas, Nenagh, Oxfam, Paddy, Portlaoise, Radi(oló), Ryanair, Telif(íli)s, Templemore, Thurles, Tipperary, Tramore, Trinity, Tr(ólo)caire, Tuam, Tullamore, Tullow, Vhi, Waterford, Youghal

For the structural markers we used more conservative query patterns where appropriate, to minimise false positives. For this reason the incidence figures given here should be considered lower estimates of the frequency of these structures, but they allow us to establish an independent metric with a minimum of manual intervention.

As mentioned above, for the emphatic use of reflexives, we searched only in the subject verb configuration, even though these are possible in other argument positions also (e.g. *I saw himself in the pub yesterday*). The query was restricted to reflexive pronouns (other than *itself*) found at the start of a sentence, or immediately after a conjunction, and directly before a finite verb (other than *have* or *be*). The CQP query (4) yields examples such as (5)-(7).

(4) [pos="CC" | pos="SENT"] [lemma=".+self" & lemma!="itself"] [pos="VV[ZD]?"];

(5) ... more commonplace or didactic, less imaginative? **Himself added**, "You are a romantic idiot, and I love you more than...

(6) ... Instruments in Lansing, Michigan, where Val and Don **and myself taught** bouzouki, mandolin, guitar and fiddle workshops. It is a...

(7) ... game of crazy golf, except this time it was outdoor. Conor **and myself got** bored straight away so we formed our own game while Mike ...

For the "after" perfective construction, we searched for a pattern of a personal pronoun (i.e. not including *it, this, that*), the lexeme *after*, and a gerund form of a common verb (other than *have, be*). The query (8) allowed for a modal auxiliary, and for intervening adverbs, as illustrated in (9)-(11).

(8) [pos="PP" & word!="it" %c & word!="that" %c & word!="this" %c] [pos="RB.*"]* [lemma="be"] [pos="RB.*"]* [word="after"] [pos="RB.*"]* [pos="V[VH]G"]

(9) ... the holy angels on your head, young fellow. I hear tell **you're after winning** all in the sports below; and wasn't it a shame I didn't ...

(10) ... MICHAEL – Is the old lad killed surely? PHILLY. **I'm after feeling** the last gasps quitting his heart. MICHAEL – Look at ...

(11) ... placards with the words "Blind as a Batt" and "Batman **you are after robbing** us". They came from as far away as Wexford and called ...

The use of embedded inversions in complements was queried for the same four verbs identified by (Kirk and Kallen, 2007): *ask*, *see*, *wonder* and *know*. Other verbs were considered, by expansion from these four via Levin verb classes (Levin, 1993), but preliminary results gave many false positives. The query used search for one of these four verbs, followed by a form of the verb *be*, and then a personal pronoun specific to the subject position (12). Examples of the instances extracted are given below (13)-(15).

(12) [pos="VV.*" & lemma="(ask|know|see|wonder)" %c] [lemma="be"] [word="(I|he|she|we|they)" %c];

(13) ... but that is the reality. I remember as a young child being **asked was I** a Protestant or a Catholic: that's the worst thing ...

(14) ... unless I get 170+, there isn't a chance. And then I **wonder am I** mad even applying for medicine. Anyway anyone else who's...

(15) There was the all important question and she was dying to **know was he** a married man or a widower who had lost his wife or some ...

Finally, examples of the *amn't* contraction (17)-(19) were extracted with the simple case-insensitive query (16).

(16) "am" "n't";

(17) Hi I'm relatively new to CCTV but work in IT and so **amn't** 100 % lost ! Anyway, I have already set up a personal ...

(18) ... and plaster, with some pride.) It was he did that, and **amn't** I a great wonder to think I 've traced him ten days with ...

(19) "I will indeed Mrs. R, thanks very much, sure **amn't** I only parchin?" Ye needn't have gone to the trouble of ...

It should be noted that these structural usages differ in the degree to which they are perceived as distinctive. While speakers of Irish English may not be aware that *amn't* and the embedded inversion construction are dialectally restricted, many do know that the *after* and reflexive constructions are particular to Ireland. Hence by searching for these constructions our evaluation is biased towards colloquial language and consciously dialectal usage.

5 Results

As can be seen in the first two rows of table 1, considerably large Irish corpora were gathered with ease, and even after applying several subsequent filtering strategies, the smallest corpus was several times the size of the manually assembled ICE-Ireland corpus.

Figure 1 (left panel) further shows that the strategy of searching by random seed combinations yielded pages in many domains, with a considerable proportion being in the .ie domain, but by no means the majority. This suggests that Ireland specific usage of English is not restricted to the national internet domain, i.e. the .ie TLD. The relative proportion of .ie domain pages (see right panel of same figure) was increased by selecting only pages which had predominantly British orthography, suggesting that this has some efficacy in eliminating texts written in American English.

Table 1 also shows the absolute incidence of each of the five characteristic phenomena considered. All matches returned by the CQP search queries were manually evaluated, to ensure that they were authentic examples of the constructions in question (for the larger ukWaC corpus only a random sample were examined). Numbers of false positives that were excluded are shown in brackets, such as the examples from ukWaC below:

(20) ... just as they were **after** receiving secret briefings from Health Commission Wales officers.

(21) All I **know is they**'re getting cold.

The bars in sets one and two show figures for the manually compiled ICE-Ireland corpus, and the Crúbadán web-corpus. The ICE-Ireland numbers differ somewhat from those reported in that paper (Kirk and Kallen, 2007), since we used more selective search strategies (note that the cut-off reported relative incidences reach about 21 per mil. tokens), which would miss some examples such as those below which have the after construction without a personal pronoun, and have the non-reflexive use in object position, respectively:

(22) There's nothing new **after** coming in anyway so

(23) Again it's up to **yourself** which type of pricing policy you use

It should also be noted that ICE-Ireland, following the standard scheme for the International Corpus of English project (Greenbaum, 1996), is biased towards spoken language, with written text only making up only 40% of the total text.

The relative incidence (per million tokens) of Ireland-specific topics and constructions is summarised in figure 2. The bars in sets three and four demonstrate that these same characteristics, very common in Hiberno-English as evidenced by the ICE-Ireland, appear to be exceedingly rare in UK and US English. Unsurprisingly, web authors in the US and UK domains do not write often about Irish places and organisations. But constructions that are putatively exclusive to Hiberno-English are seldom found. Those that are found might be explained by the effect of language contact with Irish immigrants to those countries, and the fact that text by Irish authors may be found in these domains, whether those people are resident in those countries or not. For instance in the example below, the given name *Ronan* suggests that the author might be of Irish extraction:

(24) At about that point Cardinal Cormac of Westminster walked right past us and Ronan and **myself** went to say hello to him and tell him we were up here from his diocese.

The sets headed ".ie" show the figures for the corpora we constructed by querying seed terms within the Irish national domain. The incidence of characteristic features of Hiberno-English grammar are higher than those seen in the US and UK domains, similar to that seen in the Crúbadán corpus, and lower than in the ICE-Ireland corpus, perhaps reflecting the fact that these constructions are less common in written Hiberno-English. Subsequent filtering out of pages with dominance of American English spelling (".ie, BrEn") does not have much effect on the numbers.

The "Irish Seeds (IEs)" bars show that the use of tailored seed terms returns text which has a similar topical specificity to that in the .ie domain generally, but which shows more structural characteristics of Hiberno-English. These results can also be improved upon, first by concentrating on the .ie domain portion of the tailored-seeds extracted pages ("Irish Seeds (IEs), IE Dom (.ie)") which boosts topical specificity. Filtering instead by orthography ("IEs, BrEn") seems to strike a happy medium, increasing incidence in all categories.

However returning to table 1, it is apparent that there are many false positives among the constructions found using Irish seed terms. This was caused by the search strategy retrieving a small number of pages on the topic of Hiberno-English, that contained many constructed examples of the structures of interest. The same corpora contained smaller numbers of examples from theatre scripts and other fiction.

6 Discussion

The results show us that our methods can be effective in extracting text that is both specific to Irish topics, and includes instances of constructions that are particular to the variety of English spoken in Ireland. The incidences relative to corpus size are not as high as those seen in the

Table 1: Corpora sizes, incidences of Ireland terms and constructions; absolute numbers (false positives in brackets)

	ICE-Ireland	Crubadan	ukWaC	UKs, 3T, .us	UKs, 3T, .ie	UKs, 3T, .ie, BrEn	IEs, 3T, .ALL	IEs, 3T, .ALL, .ie	IEs, 3T, .ALL, BrEn	IEs, 2T, .ALL	IEs, 2T, .ie
Size (in 10^6 Tokens)	1.1	46.3	2119.9	74.7	17.8	15.0	25.2	2.6	17.3	18.4	6.4
Size (in 10^3 Docs)	0.5	43.0	2692.6	4.6	2.0	1.6	3.4	0.7	2.5	7.3	2.3
Ireland Terms	194	17330	12743	82	14199	13802	23527	7264	22071	12454	9935
"after" Construction	7 (-4)	12 (2)	48 (72)	1 (2)	11 (1)	7 (1)	26 (50)	2 (1)	11 (47)	14 (38)	9 (1)
"amn't" Construction	0 (0)	0 (0)	32 (0)	0 (0)	0 (0)	0 (0)	5 (45)	1 (1)	2 (43)	6 (36)	0 (0)
embedded Inversions	24 (-18)	18 (5)	42 (309)	0 (15)	5 (2)	5 (0)	20 (4)	2 (1)	17 (2)	4 (1)	5 (0)
Subject Reflexives	22 (-19)	33 (0)	1797 (115)	35 (8)	15 (1)	10 (0)	39 (0)	2 (0)	30 (0)	17 (3)	8 (1)

Figure 1: Domain composition of Irish-Seed based Corpora

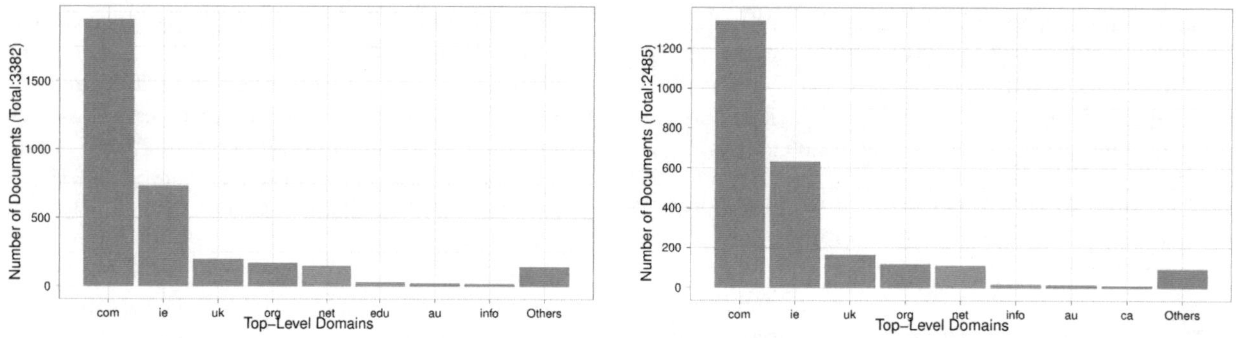

Figure 2: Relative Incidences of Ireland terms and constructions, per million words (grey bars indicating the original counts before manual inspection), in each copus

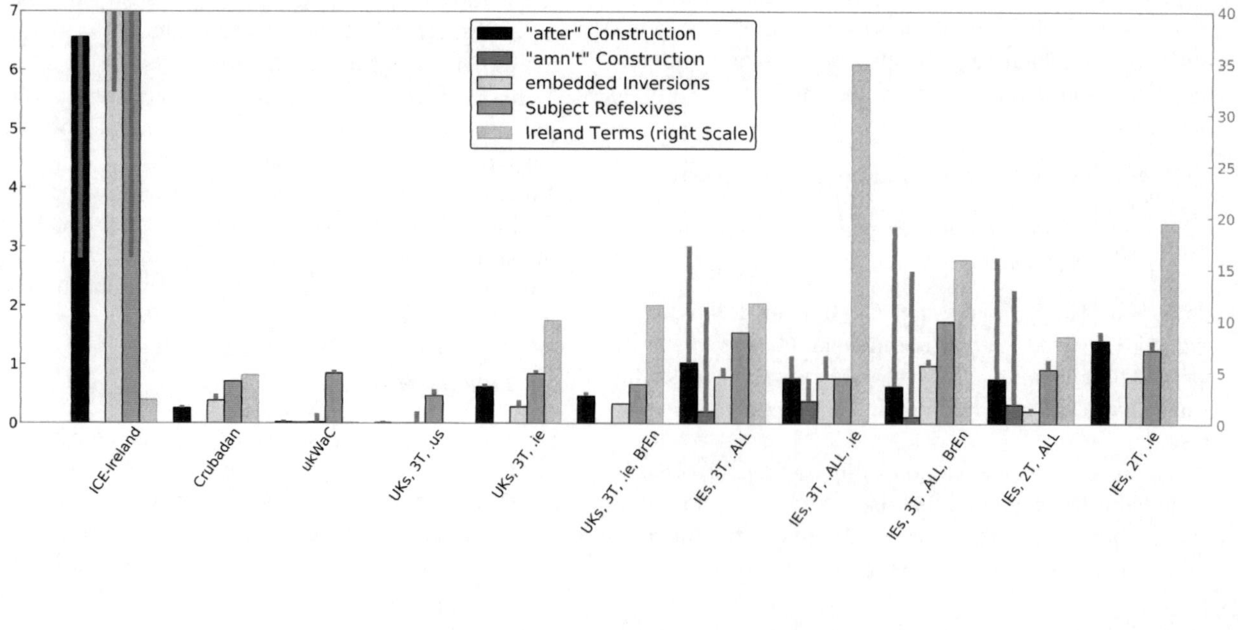

manually constructed ICE-Ireland corpus. We can speculate on the reasons for this. It may be in part due to "pollution" of our corpus with non-Irish English, via syndicated journalism (e.g. some Irish newspapers are repackaging of British newspapers with added Irish content), or via multinational organisations with bases in Ireland. In our view the main explanatory factor is that of modality and register. The ICE-Ireland corpus is predominantly spoken (~60%), with many texts coming from informal settings (unscripted speeches, face to face and telephone conversations). One reading of the figures which is consistent with this viewpoint is that the .ie domain corpora contain proportionally more high register, edited text (e.g. from governmental and commercial organisations, for which the use of the .ie domain may be an important part of corporate identity), and that the tailored-seed corpora contain more text contributed by individuals (forums, blogs, etc), for whom domain endings are of little consequence. Nevertheless, the use of Hiberno-English specific seed terms did reveal higher incidences of distinctive Irish usages than simple domain filtering.

But despite these lower incidences, in absolute terms our corpora provide many more examples of Hiberno-English than that were hitherto available. For example the ICE-Ireland corpus contains a total of seven examples of the "after" construction, while with our Irish-seeds derived corpus, and using a fairly restrictive query pattern, we isolated 26 examples of this structure. Further the size of these pilot corpora were kept intentionally limited, a small fraction of the approximately 150 million .ie domain pages indexed by Google. Much larger corpora could be constructed with relative ease, by using a larger seed set, or with an interactive seed-discovery method, where the text from the first round of web-harvesting could be analysed to identify further terms that are comparatively specific to Hiberno-English (relative to corpora of other varieties of English), in a similar fashion to the methods discussed in (Scannell, 2007).

In terms of wider implications, the fact that seeds tailored to a particular region and language variant is as effective as filtering by domain, is encouraging for dialects and minority languages that lack a dedicated internet domain. This suggest that for less-dominant language variants without distinctive established orthographies (e.g. Scots, Andalusian, Bavarian), large corpora displaying characteristic features of that variant can be constructed in a simple automatic manner with minimal supervision (a small set of seeds provided by native speakers). Our methods might also prove useful for dialects in which a standard variant is dominant in the written language (e.g. Arabic, Chinese). One might expect that the written Arabic in the .ma (Morocco) domain would differ little from that in the .qa domain (Qatar) despite the large differences in vernacular speech. Similarly the grammar and vocabulary of Chinese written in Mainland Chinese, Taiwanese, Hong Kong and Singaporese domains (ignoring orthography) might be less representative of the variation in everyday language. The use of regional slang and proper names may help one to collect more examples of this more natural language usage, and less of the dominant standard variant.

References

Baroni, M. and Bernardini, S. (2004). BootCaT: Bootstrapping corpora and terms from the web. In (ELRA), E. L. R. A., editor, *Proceedings of LREC 2004, Lisbon: ELDA.*, pages 1313–1316.

Baroni, M. and Bernardini, S., editors (2006). *Wacky! Working papers on the Web as Corpus.*

Baroni, M., Bernardini, S., Ferraresi, A., and Zanchetta, E. (2009). The WaCky wide web: a collection of very large linguistically processed web-crawled corpora. *Language Resources and Evaluation*, 43(3):209–226.

Burnard, L. (1995). *Users Reference Guide, British National Corpus, Version 1.0.* Oxford University Computing Services/British National Corpus Consortium, Oxford.

Christ, O. (1994). A Modular and Flexible Architecture for an Integrated Corpus Query System. In *Papers in Computational Lexicography (COMPLEX '94)*, pages 22–32.

Erjavec, I. S., Erjavec, T., and Kilgarriff, A. (2008). A web corpus and word sketches for Japanese. *Information and Media Technologies*, 3:529–551.

Finn, A., Kushmerick, N., and Smyth, B. (2001). Fact or fiction: Content classification for digital libraries.

Greenbaum, S. (1996). *Comparing English Worldwide.* Clarendon Press.

Guevara, E. (2010). NoWaC: a large web-based corpus for Norwegian. In *Proceedings of the Sixth Web as Corpus Workshop (WAC6)*, pages 1–7. The Association for Computational Linguistics.

Kallen, J. and Kirk, J. (2007). ICE-Ireland: Local variations on global standards. In Beal, J. C., Corrigan, K. P., and Moisl, H. L., editors, *Creating and Digitizing Language Corpora: Synchronic Databases*, volume 1, pages 121–162. Palgrave Macmillan, London.

Kirk, J. and Kallen, J. (2007). Assessing Celticity in a Corpus of Irish Standard English. In *The Celtic languages in contact: papers from the workshop within the framework of the XIII International Congress of Celtic Studies, Bonn, 26-27 July 2007*, page 270.

Levin, B. (1993). *English Verb Classes and Alternations.* University of Chicago Press, Chicago.

Nelson, G., Wallis, S., and Aarts, B. (2002). *Exploring natural language: working with the British component of the International Corpus of English.* John Benjamins.

Scannell, K. (2007). The Crúbadán project: Corpus building for under-resourced languages. In Fairon, C., Naets, H., Kilgarriff, A., and de Schryver, G.-M., editors, *Building and Exploring Web Corpora: Proceedings of the 3rd Web as Corpus Workshop*, volume 4, pages 5–15.

Web (2008). The IMS Open Corpus Workbench (CWB).

Yahoo! Inc. (1995). The Yahoo! Internet search engine.

Syntactic transformations for Swiss German dialects

Yves Scherrer
LATL
Université de Genève
Geneva, Switzerland
yves.scherrer@unige.ch

Abstract

While most dialectological research so far focuses on phonetic and lexical phenomena, we use recent fieldwork in the domain of dialect syntax to guide the development of multidialectal natural language processing tools. In particular, we develop a set of rules that transform Standard German sentence structures into syntactically valid Swiss German sentence structures. These rules are sensitive to the dialect area, so that the dialects of more than 300 towns are covered. We evaluate the transformation rules on a Standard German treebank and obtain accuracy figures of 85% and above for most rules. We analyze the most frequent errors and discuss the benefit of these transformations for various natural language processing tasks.

1 Introduction

For over a century, dialectological research has focused on phonetic, lexical and morphological phenomena. It is only recently, since the 1990s, that syntax has gained the attraction of dialectologists. As a result, syntactic data from field studies are now available for many dialect areas. This paper explores how dialect syntax fieldwork can guide the development of multidialectal natural language processing tools. Our goal is to transform Standard German sentence structures so that they become syntactically valid in Swiss German dialects.[1]

These transformations are accomplished by a set of hand-crafted rules, developed and evaluated on the basis of the dependency version of the Standard German TIGER treebank. Ultimately, the rule set can be used either as a tool for treebank transduction (i.e. deriving Swiss German treebanks from Standard German ones), or as the syntactic transfer module of a transfer-based machine translation system.

After the discussion of related work (Section 2), we present the major syntactic differences between Standard German and Swiss German dialects (Section 3). We then show how these differences can be covered by a set of transformation rules that apply to syntactically annotated Standard German text, such as found in treebanks (Section 4). In Section 5, we give some coverage figures and discuss the most common errors that result from these transformations. We conclude in Section 6.

2 Related work

One line of research in natural language processing deals with parsing methods for dialects. Chiang et al. (2006) argue that it is often easier to manually create resources that relate a dialect to a standard language than it is to manually create syntactically annotated resources for the dialect itself. They investigate three approaches for parsing the Levantine dialect of Arabic, one of which consists of transducing a Standard Arabic treebank into Levantine with the help of hand-crafted rules. We agree with this point of view: we devise transformation rules that relate Swiss German dialects to Standard German.

In the case of closely related languages,[2] different

[1] Here, we do not take into account the phonetic, morphological and lexical changes involved in generating the actual Swiss German word forms. For such a model, see for example Scherrer and Rambow (2010a).

[2] In any case, it is difficult to establish strict linguistic criteria

Proceedings of EMNLP 2011, Conference on Empirical Methods in Natural Language Processing, pages 30–38,
Edinburgh, Scotland, UK, July 27–31, 2011.

types of annotation projection have been proposed to facilitate the creation of treebanks. See Volk and Samuelsson (2004) for an overview of the problem.

In a rather different approach, Vaillant (2008) presents a hand-crafted multi-dialect grammar that conceives of a dialect as some kind of "agreement feature". This allows to share identical rules across dialects and differentiate them only where necessary. We follow a similar approach by linking the transformation rules to geographical data from recent dialectological fieldwork.

Another line of research is oriented towards machine translation models for closely related languages. It is common in this field that minor syntactic differences are dealt with explicitly. Corbí-Bellot et al. (2005) present a shallow-transfer system for the different Romance languages of Spain. Structural transfer rules account for gender change and word reorderings. Another system (Homola and Kuboň, 2005) covers several Slavonic languages of Eastern Europe and confirms the necessity of shallow parsing except for the most similar language pair (Czech-Slovak).

In contrast, statistical machine translation systems have been proposed to translate closely related languages on a letter-by-letter basis (Vilar et al., 2007; Tiedemann, 2009). However, the word reordering capabilities of a common phrase-based model are still required to obtain reasonable performances.

3 The main syntactic features of Swiss German dialects

A general description of the linguistic particularities of Swiss German dialects, including syntax, can be found, for example, in Lötscher (1983). Some syntactic case studies within the framework of Generative Grammar are presented in Penner (1995). Currently, a dialectological survey, under the name of SADS (*Syntaktischer Atlas der deutschen Schweiz*), aims at producing a syntactic atlas of German-speaking Switzerland (Bucheli and Glaser, 2002). Some preliminary results of this project are described in Klausmann (2006).[3]

There are two main types of syntactic differences between Swiss German dialects and Standard German. Some of the differences are representative of the mainly spoken use of Swiss German. They do not show much interdialectal variation, and they are also encountered in other spoken varieties of German. Other differences are dialectological in nature, in the sense that they are specific to some subgroups of Swiss German dialects and usually do not occur outside of the Alemannic dialect group. This second type of differences constitutes the main research object of the SADS project. In the following subsections, we will show some examples of both types of phenomena.

3.1 Features of spoken language

No preterite tense Swiss German dialects do not have synthetic preterite forms and use (analytic) perfect forms instead (1a).[4] Transforming a Standard German preterite form is not trivial: the correct auxiliary verb and participle forms have to be generated, and they have to be inserted at the correct place (in the right verb bracket).

Standard German pluperfect is handled in the same way: the inflected preterite auxiliary verb is transformed into an inflected present auxiliary verb and an auxiliary participle, while the participle of the main verb is retained (1b). The resulting construction is called double perfect.

(1) a. Wir gingen ins Kino.
→ Wir sind ins Kino gegangen.
'We went to the cinema.'

b. als er gegangen war
→ als er gegangen gewesen ist
'when he had gone'

No genitive case Standard German genitive case is replaced by different means in Swiss German. Some prepositions (e.g. *wegen, während* 'because, during') use dative case instead of genitive. Other prepositions become complex through the addition of a second preposition *von* (e.g. *innerhalb* 'within'). Verbs requiring a genitive object in Standard German generally use a dative object in Swiss

to distinguish "dialects" from "closely related languages".

[3]We thank Elvira Glaser and her team for providing us access to the SADS database. This work could not have been carried out without these precious data.

[4]Throughout this paper, the examples are given with Standard German words, but Swiss German word order. We hope that this simplifies the reading for Standard German speakers.

German unless they are lexically replaced. Genitive appositions are converted to PPs with *von* 'of' in the case of non-human NPs (2a), or to a dative-possessive construction with human NPs (2b).

(2) a. der Schatzmeister der Partei
→ der Schatzmeister von der Partei
'the treasurer of the party'
b. das Haus des Lehrers
→ dem Lehrer sein Haus
'the teacher's house',
litt. 'to the teacher his house'

Determiners with person names A third difference is the prevalent use of person names with determiners, whereas (written) Standard German avoids determiners in this context:

(3) a. Hans → der Hans 'Hans'
b. Frau Müller → die Frau Müller 'Miss M.'

3.2 Dialect-specific features

Verb raising When two or more verbal forms appear in the right verb bracket, their order is often reversed with respect to Standard German. Several cases exist. In Western Swiss dialects, the auxiliary verb may precede the participle in subordinate clauses (4a). In all but Southeastern dialects, the modal verb precedes the infinitive (4b).

Verb raising also occurs for full verbs with infinitival complements, like *lassen* 'to let' (4c). In this case, the dependencies between *lassen* and its complements cross those between the main verb and its complements:

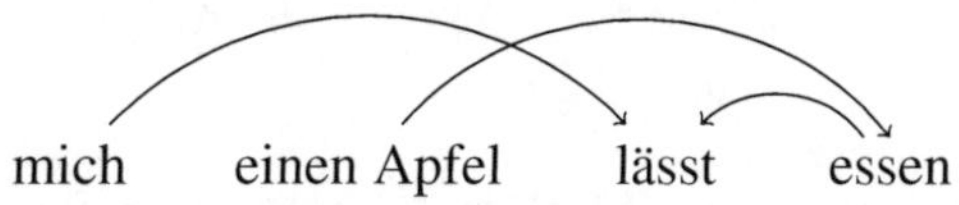

Verb projection raising In the same contexts as above, the main verb extraposes to the right along with its complements (4d), (4e).

(4) a. dass er gegangen ist
→ dass er ist gegangen
'that he has gone'
b. dass du einen Apfel essen willst
→ dass du einen Apfel willst essen
'that you want to eat an apple'
c. dass du mich einen Apfel essen lässt
→ dass du mich einen Apfel lässt essen
'that you let me eat an apple'
d. dass du einen Apfel essen willst
→ dass du willst einen Apfel essen
'that you want to eat an apple'
e. dass du mich einen Apfel essen lässt
→ dass du mich lässt einen Apfel essen
'that you let me eat an apple'

Prepositional dative marking In Central Swiss dialects, dative objects are introduced by a dummy preposition *i* or *a* (5a). However, this preposition is not added if the dative noun phrase is already part of a prepositional phrase (5b).

(5) a. der Mutter → i/a der Mutter
'the mother (dative)'
b. mit der Mutter → mit (*i/a) der Mutter
'with the mother'

Article doubling In adjective phrases that contain an intensity adverb like *ganz, so* 'very, such', the determiner occurs either before the adverb as in Standard German, or after the adverb, or in both positions, depending on the dialect:

(6) ein ganz lieber Mann
→ ganz ein lieber Mann
→ ein ganz ein lieber Mann
'a very dear man'

Complementizer in wh-phrases Interrogative subordinate clauses introduced by verbs like *fragen* 'to ask' may see the complementizer *dass* attached after the interrogative adverb or pronoun.

Relative pronouns Nominative and accusative relative pronouns are substituted in most Swiss German dialects by the uninflected particle *wo*. In dative (7a) or prepositional (7b) contexts, the particle *wo* appears together with an inflected personal pronoun:

(7) a. dem → wo ... ihm
b. mit dem → wo ... mit ihm, wo ... damit

Final clauses Standard German allows non-finite final clauses with the complementizer *um ... zu* 'in order to'. In Western dialects, this complementizer is rendered as *für ... z*. In Eastern dialects, a single particle *zum* is used. An intermediate form *zum ... z* also exists.

Pronoun sequences In a sequence of accusative and dative pronouns, the accusative usually precedes in Standard German, whereas the dative precedes in many Swiss German dialects:

(8) es ihm → ihm es 'it to him'

Predicative adjectives In Southwestern dialects, predicative adjectives agree in gender and number with the subject:

(9) er / sie / es ist alt
→ er / sie / es ist alter / alte / altes
'he / she / it is old'

Copredicative adjectives A slightly different problem is the agreement of copredicative adjectives. A copredicative adjective[5] relates as an attribute to a noun phrase, but also to the predicate of the sentence (see example below). In Northeastern dialects, there is an invariable *er*-ending[6] for all genders and numbers. In Southern dialects, the copredicative adjective agrees in gender and number. Elsewhere, the uninflected adjective form is used, as in Standard German.

(10) Sie sollten die Milch warm trinken.
→ Sie sollten die Milch warme$_{\text{Fem.Sg}}$ / warmer$_{\text{Invar}}$ trinken.
'You should drink the milk warm.'

3.3 The SADS data

The SADS survey consists of four written questionnaires, each of which comprises about 30 questions about syntactic phenomena like the ones cited above. They were submitted to 3185 informants in 383 inquiry points.[7] For each question, the informants were asked to write down the variant(s) that they deemed acceptable in their dialect.

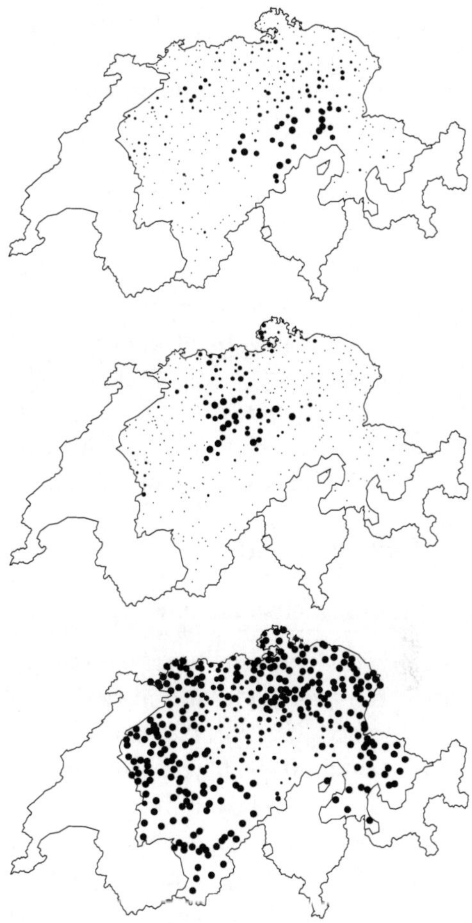

Figure 1: The three maps show the geographical distribution of prepositional dative marking with *a* (top) and with *i* (center). The bottom map shows the inquiry points in which no preposition is added to dative NPs. The maps are based on SADS question I/7. Larger circles represent larger proportions of informants considering the respective variant as the most natural one.

The SADS data give us an overview of the syntactic phenomena and their variants occurring in the different Swiss German dialects. It is on the basis of these data that we compiled the list of phenomena presented above. More importantly, the SADS data provide us with a mapping from variants to inquiry points. It suffices thus to implement a small number of variants (between 1 and 5 for a typical phenomenon) to obtain full coverage of the 383 inquiry points. Figure 1 shows the geographical distribution of the three variants of prepositional dative marking.

For a subset of syntactic phenomena, two types of questions were asked:

[5]This phenomenon is also known as *depictive secondary predicate construction*.

[6]This (reconstructed) ending is thought to be a frozen masculine inflection marker; in practice, it is pronounced [ə] or [a] in the corresponding dialects.

[7]`http://www.ds.uzh.ch/dialektsyntax/eckdaten.html`, accessed 8.6.2011.

- Which variants are acceptable in your dialect?
- Which variant do you consider the most natural one in your dialect?

In the first case, multiple mentions were allowed. Usually, dialect speakers are very tolerant in accepting also variants that they would not naturally utter themselves. In this sense, the first set of questions can be conceived as a geographical model of dialect perception, while the second set of questions rather yields a geographical model of dialect production. According to the task at hand, the transformation rules can be used with either one of the data sets.

4 Transformation rules

4.1 The Standard German corpus

The transformation rules require morphosyntactically annotated Standard German input data. Therefore, we had to choose a specific annotation format and a specific corpus to test the rules on. We selected the Standard German TIGER treebank (Brants et al., 2002), in the CoNLL-style dependency format (Buchholz and Marsi, 2006; Kübler, 2008).[8] This format allows a compact representation of the syntactic structure. Figure 2 shows a sample sentence, annotated in this format.

While we use the TIGER corpus for test and evaluation purposes in this paper, the rules are aimed to be sufficiently generic so that they apply correctly to any other corpus annotated according to the same guidelines.

4.2 Rule implementation

We have manually created transformation rules for a dozen of syntactic and morphosyntactic phenomena. These rules (i) detect a specific syntactic pattern in a sentence and (ii) modify the position, content and/or dependency link of the nodes in that pattern. The rules are implemented in the form of Python scripts.

As an example, let us describe the transformation rule for article doubling. This rule detects the following syntactic pattern:[9]

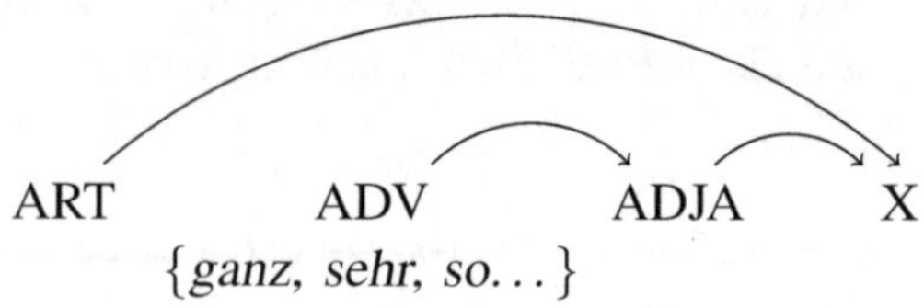

The rule then produces the three valid Swiss German patterns – as said above, the transformation rules may yield different output structures for different dialects. One of the three variants is identical to the Standard German structure produced above. In a second variant, the positions of the article and the adverb are exchanged without modifying the dependency links:

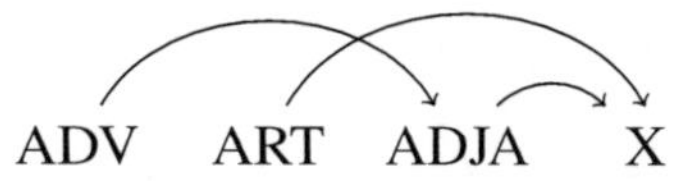

This transformation yields non-projective dependencies (i.e. crossing arcs), which are problematic for some parsing algorithms. However, the original TIGER annotations already contain non-projective dependencies. Thus, there is no additional complexity involved in the resulting Swiss German structures.

The third variant contains two occurrences of the determiner, before and after the intensity adverb. We chose to make both occurrences dependents of the same head node:

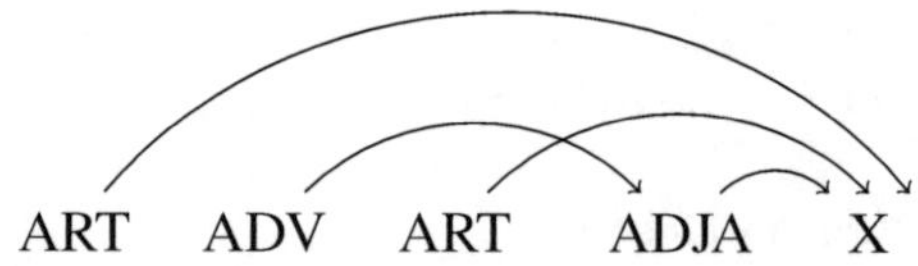

As mentioned previously, the SADS data tell us which of the three variants is accepted in which of the 384 inquiry points. This mapping is non-deterministic: more than one variant may be accepted at a given inquiry point.

5 Evaluation

5.1 Corpus frequencies

In order to get an idea of the frequency of the syntactic constructions mentioned in Section 3, we started by searching the TIGER treebank for the crucial syntactic patterns. Table 1 shows frequency counts

[8] Thanks to Yannick Versley for making this version available to us.

[9] X symbolizes any type of node that possesses an article and an adjective as dependents. In practice, X usually is a noun.

ID	FORM	LEMMA	CPOSTAG	POSTAG	FEATS	HEAD	DEPREL
1	für	für	APPR	PREP	–	4	PP
2	eine	eine	ART	ART	Acc.Sg.Fem	3	DET
3	Statistik	Statistik	NN	N	Acc.Sg.Fem	1	PN
4	reicht	reichen	VVFIN	V	3.Sg.Pres.Ind	0	ROOT
5	das	das	PDS	PRO	Nom.Sg.Neut	4	SUBJ
6	nicht	nicht	PTKNEG	PTKNEG	–	4	ADV
7	.	.	$.	$.	–	0	ROOT

Figure 2: Example of a CoNLL-style annotated sentence. Each word (FORM) is numbered (ID), lemmatized (LEMMA), annotated with two levels of part-of-speech tags (CPOSTAG and POSTAG), annotated with morphological information (FEATS) and with dependency relations. HEAD indicates the ID of the head word, and DEPREL indicates the type of dependency relation. For example, the word at position 1 (*für*) depends on the word at position 4 (*reicht*) by a PP relation.

Construction	Sentences
Preterite tense	13439
Genitive case	15351
Person name determiners	5410
Verb raising	3246
Verb projection raising	2597
Prep. dative marking	2708
Article doubling	61
Compl. in wh-phrases	478
Relative pronouns	4619
Final clauses	629
Pronoun sequences	6
Predicative adjectives	2784
Total TIGER sentences	40000

Table 1: Number of sentences in the TIGER corpus that trigger the mentioned transformation rule.

of the respective phenomena.[10]

This preliminary study led us to exclude phenomena that could not be detected reliably because the morphosyntactic annotations in TIGER were not precise enough. For example, TIGER does not distinguish between copredicative (11a) and adverbial (11b) uses of adjectives. Therefore, it is impossible to automatically count the number of copredicative adjectives, let alone perform the necessary dialectal transformations.

[10]These figures should be taken with a grain of salt. First, the TIGER corpus consists of newspaper text, which is hardly representative of everyday use of Swiss German dialects. Second, it is difficult to obtain reliable recall figures without manually inspecting the entire corpus.

(11) a. Blitzblank hängen die Töpfe an der Küchenwand.
'The pots are hanging sparkling clean on the kitchen wall.'

b. Häufig hängen die Töpfe an der Küchenwand.
'The pots frequently hang on the kitchen wall.'

5.2 Results

For each syntactic construction, a development set and a test set were extracted from the TIGER treebank, each of them comprising at most 100 sentences showing that construction. After achieving fair performance on the development sets, the held-out test data was manually evaluated.

We did not evaluate the accusative-dative pronoun sequences because of their small number of occurrences. Predicative adjective agreement was not evaluated because the author did not have native speaker's intuitions about this phenomenon.

Table 2 shows the accuracy of the rules on the test data. Recall that some rules cover different dialectal variants, each of which may show different types of errors. In consequence, the performance of some rules is indicated as an interval. Moreover, some dialectal variants do not require any syntactic change of the Standard German source, yielding figures of 100% accuracy.

The evaluation was performed on variants, not on inquiry points. The mapping between the variants and the inquiry points is supported by the SADS data and is not the object of the present evaluation.

Construction	Accuracy
Preterite tense	89%
Genitive case	85–93%
Person name determiners	80%
Verb raising	96–100%
Verb projection raising	85–100%
Prep. dative marking	93–100%
Article doubling	100%
Compl. in wh-phrases	69–100%
Relative pronouns	86–99%
Final clauses	92–100%

Table 2: This table shows the accuracy of the transformations, manually evaluated on the test set.

The overall performance of the transformation rules lies at 85% accuracy and above for most rules. Four major error types can be distinguished.

Annotation errors The annotation of the TIGER treebank has been done semi-automatically and is not exempt of errors, especially in the case of out-of-vocabulary words. These problems degrade the performance of rules dealing with proper nouns. In (12), the first name *Traute* is wrongly analyzed as a preterite verb form *traute* 'trusted, wedded', leading to an erroneous placement of the determiner.

(12) Traute Müller
→ *traute die Müller / die Traute Müller

Imperfect heuristics Some rules rely on a syntactic distinction that is not explicitly encoded in the TIGER annotation. Therefore, we had to resort to heuristics, which do not work well in all cases. For example, the genitive replacement rule needs to distinguish human from non-human NPs. Likewise, adding a complementizer to wh-phrases overgenerates because the TIGER annotation does not reliably distinguish between clause-adjoined relative clauses and interrogative clauses introduced as complement of the main verb.

Conjunctions Many rules rely on the dependency relation type (the DEPREL field in Figure 2). According to the CoNLL guidelines, the dependency type is only encoded in the first conjunct of a conjunction, but not in the second. As a result, the transformations are often only applied to the first conjunct. However, it should not be too difficult to handle the most frequent types of conjunctions.

Word order errors Appositions and quotation marks sometimes interfere with transformation rules and lead to typographically or syntactically unfortunate sentences. In other cases, the linguistic description is not very explicit. For example, in the verb projection raising rule, we found it difficult to decide which constituents are moved and which are not. Moving polarity items is sometimes blocked due to scope effects. Different types of adverbs also tend to behave differently.

5.3 An example

In the previous section, we evaluated each syntactic transformation rule individually. It is also possible to apply all rules in cascade. The following example shows an original Standard German sentence (13a) along with three dialectal variants, obtained by the cascaded application of our transformation rules. The Mörschwil dialect (Northeastern Switzerland, Canton St. Gallen) shows genitive replacement and relative pronoun replacement (13b). The Central Swiss dialect of Sempach (Canton Lucerne) additionally shows prepositional dative marking (13c), while the Guttannen dialect (Southwestern Switzerland, Canton Berne) shows an instance of verb raising (13d). All transformations are underlined. Note again that the transformation rules only produce Swiss German morphosyntactic structures, but do not include word-level adaptations. For illustration, the last example (13e) includes word-level translations and corresponds thus to the "real" dialect spoken in Mörschwil.

(13) a. **Original:** Einen besonderen Stellenwert verdient dabei die alarmierende Zahl junger Menschen, die der PDS ihre Stimme gegeben haben.
'Special importance should be paid to the alarming number of young people who have given their vote to the PDS.'

b. **Mörschwil:** Einen besonderen Stellenwert verdient dabei die alarmierende Zahl von jungen Menschen, wo der PDS ihre Stimme gegeben haben.

c. **Sempach:** Einen besonderen Stellenwert verdient dabei die alarmierende Zahl von jungen Menschen, wo i der PDS ihre Stimme gegeben haben.

d. **Guttannen:** Einen besonderen Stellenwert verdient dabei die alarmierende Zahl von jungen Menschen, wo der PDS ihre Stimme haben gegeben.

e. **Mörschwil ("real"):** En bsondere Stellewert vedient debii di alarmierend Zahl vo junge Mensche, wo de PDS iri Stimm ggee hend.

6 Conclusion and future work

We have shown that a small number of manually written transformation rules can model the most important syntactic differences between Standard German and Swiss German dialects with high levels of accuracy. Data of recent dialectological fieldwork provides us with a list of relevant phenomena and their respective geographic distribution patterns, so that we are able to devise the unique combination of transformation rules for more than 300 inquiry points.

A large part of current work in natural language processing deals with inferring linguistic structures from raw textual data. In our setting, this work has already been done by the dialectologists: by devising questionnaires of the most important syntactic phenomena, collecting data from native dialect speakers and synthesizing the results of the survey in the form of a database. Relying on this work allows us to obtain precise results for a great variety of dialects, where machine learning techniques would likely run into data sparseness issues.

The major limitation we found with our approach is the lacking precision (for our purposes) of the Standard German treebank annotation. Indeed, some of the syntactic distinctions that are made in Swiss German dialects are not relevant from a purely Standard German point of view, and have therefore not been distinguished in the annotation. Additional annotation could be added with the help of semantic heuristics. For example, in the case of copredicative adjectives (11), a semantic resource could easily tell that pots can be sparkling clean but not frequent.

The purpose of our work is twofold. First, the rule set can be viewed as part of a transfer-based machine translation system from Standard German to Swiss German dialects. In this case, one could use a parser to analyze any Standard German sentence before applying the transformation rules. Second, the rules allow to transform the manually annotated sentences of a Standard German treebank in order to automatically derive Swiss German treebanks. Such treebanks – even if they are of lower quality than manually annotated ones – could then be used to train statistical models for Swiss German part-of-speech tagging or full parsing. Moreover, they could be used to train statistical machine translation models to translate out of the dialects into Standard German.[11]

Both lines of research will be tested in future work. In addition, the rules presented here only deal with syntactic transformations. Word-level transformations (phonetic, lexical and morphological adaptations) will have to be dealt with by other means.

Furthermore, we would like to test if syntactic patterns can be used successfully for dialect identification, as this has been done with lexical and phonetic cues in previous work (Scherrer and Rambow, 2010b).

Another aspect of future research concerns the type of treebank used. The TIGER corpus consists of newspaper texts, which is hardly a genre frequently used in Swiss German. Spoken language texts would be more realistic to translate. The TüBa-D/S treebank (Hinrichs et al., 2000) provides syntactically annotated speech data, but its lack of morphological annotation and its diverging annotation standard have prevented its use in our research for the time being.

References

Sabine Brants, Stefanie Dipper, Silvia Hansen, Wolfgang Lezius, and George Smith. 2002. The TIGER Treebank. In *Proceedings of the Workshop on Treebanks and Linguistic Theories*, Sozopol.

Claudia Bucheli and Elvira Glaser. 2002. The syntactic atlas of Swiss German dialects: empirical and

[11] While nearly all speakers of Swiss German also understand Standard German, the inverse is not the case. Hence, a machine translation system would be most useful for the dialect-to-standard direction. The lack of parallel training data and syntactic resources for the dialect side prevented the creation of such a system until now.

methodological problems. In Sjef Barbiers, Leonie Cornips, and Susanne van der Kleij, editors, *Syntactic Microvariation*, volume II. Meertens Institute Electronic Publications in Linguistics, Amsterdam.

Sabine Buchholz and Erwin Marsi. 2006. CoNLL-X shared task on multilingual dependency parsing. In *Proceedings of the 10th Conference on Computational Natural Language Learning (CoNLL-X)*, pages 149–164, New York City.

David Chiang, Mona Diab, Nizar Habash, Owen Rambow, and Safiullah Shareef. 2006. Parsing Arabic dialects. In *EACL'06: Proceedings of the Eleventh Conference of the European Chapter of the Association for Compuational Linguistics*, pages 369–376, Trento.

Antonio M. Corbí-Bellot, Mikel L. Forcada, Sergio Ortiz-Rojas, Juan Antonio Pérez-Ortiz, Gema Ramírez-Sánchez, Felipe Sánchez-Martínez, Iñaki Alegria, Aingeru Mayor, and Kepa Sarasola. 2005. An open-source shallow-transfer machine translation engine for the Romance languages of Spain. In *Proceedings of EAMT'05*, pages 79–86, Budapest.

Erhard W. Hinrichs, Julia Bartels, Yasuhiro Kawata, Valia Kordoni, and Heike Telljohann. 2000. The Tübingen treebanks for spoken German, English, and Japanese. In Wolfgang Wahlster, editor, *Verbmobil: Foundations of Speech-to-Speech Translation*. Springer, Berlin.

Petr Homola and Vladislav Kuboň. 2005. A machine translation system into a minority language. In *Proceedings of RANLP'05*, Borovets.

Hubert Klausmann, editor. 2006. *Raumstrukturen im Alemannischen*. Neugebauer, Graz/Feldkirch.

Sandra Kübler. 2008. The PaGe 2008 shared task on parsing German. In *Proceedings of the Workshop on Parsing German*, pages 55–63, Columbus, Ohio.

Andreas Lötscher. 1983. *Schweizerdeutsch. Geschichte, Dialekte, Gebrauch*. Huber, Frauenfeld.

Zvi Penner, editor. 1995. *Topics in Swiss German Syntax*. Peter Lang, Bern.

Yves Scherrer and Owen Rambow. 2010a. Natural language processing for the Swiss German dialect area. In *Proceedings of KONVENS'10*, Saarbrücken.

Yves Scherrer and Owen Rambow. 2010b. Word-based dialect identification with georeferenced rules. In *Proceedings of EMNLP 2010*, Cambridge, MA.

Jörg Tiedemann. 2009. Character-based PSMT for closely related languages. In *Proceedings of EAMT'09*, pages 12 – 19, Barcelona.

Pascal Vaillant. 2008. A layered grammar model: Using tree-adjoining grammars to build a common syntactic kernel for related dialects. In *TAG+9 2008 – The Ninth International Workshop on Tree Adjoining Grammars and Related Formalisms*, pages 157–164, Tübingen.

David Vilar, Jan-Thorsten Peter, and Hermann Ney. 2007. Can we translate letters? In *Proceedings of the Second Workshop on Statistical Machine Translation*, pages 33–39, Prague.

Martin Volk and Yvonne Samuelsson. 2004. Bootstrapping parallel treebanks. In *COLING 2004 5th International Workshop on Linguistically Interpreted Corpora*, pages 63–70, Geneva.

Learning word-level dialectal variation as phonological replacement rules using a limited parallel corpus

Mans Hulden
University of Helsinki
Language Technology
mans.hulden@helsinki.fi

Iñaki Alegria
IXA taldea
UPV-EHU
i.alegria@ehu.es

Izaskun Etxeberria
IXA taldea
UPV-EHU
izaskun.etxeberria@ehu.es

Montse Maritxalar
IXA taldea
UPV-EHU
montse.maritxalar@ehu.es

Abstract

This paper explores two different methods of learning dialectal morphology from a small parallel corpus of standard and dialect-form text, given that a computational description of the standard morphology is available. The goal is to produce a model that translates individual lexical dialectal items to their standard dialect counterparts in order to facilitate dialectal use of available NLP tools that only assume standard-form input. The results show that a learning method based on inductive logic programming quickly converges to the correct model with respect to many phonological and morphological differences that are regular in nature.

1 Introduction

In our work with the Basque language, a morphological description and analyzer is available for the standard language, along with other tools for processing the language (Alegria et al., 2002). However, it would be convenient to be able to analyze variants and dialectal forms as well. As the dialectal differences within the Basque language are largely lexical and morphophonological, analyzing the dialectal forms would in effect require a separate morphological analyzer that is able to handle the unique lexical items in the dialect together with the differing affixes and phonological changes.

Morphological analyzers are traditionally handwritten by linguists, most commonly using some variant of the popular finite-state morphology approach (Beesley and Karttunen, 2002). This entails having an expert model a lexicon, inflectional and derivational paradigms as well as phonological alternations, and then producing a morphological analyzer/generator in the form of a finite-state transducer.

As the development of such wide-coverage morphological analyzers is labor-intesive, the hope is that an analyzer for a variant could be automatically learned from a limited parallel standard/dialect corpus, given that an analyzer already exists for the standard language. This is an interesting problem because a good solution to it could be applied to many other tasks as well: to enhancing access to digital libraries (containing diachronic and dialectal variants), for example, or to improving treatment of informal registers such as SMS messages and blogs, etc.

In this paper we evaluate two methods of learning a model from a standard/variant parallel corpus that translates a given word of the dialect to its standard-form equivalent. Both methods are based on finite-state phonology. The variant we use for experiments is Lapurdian,[1] a dialect of Basque spoken in the Lapurdi (fr. Labourd) region in the Basque Country.

Because Basque is an agglutinative, highly inflected language, we believe some of the results can be extrapolated to many other languages facing similar challenges.

One of the motivations for the current work is that there are a large number of NLP tools available and in development for standard Basque (also called Batua): a morphological analyzer, a POS tagger, a dependency analyzer, an MT engine, among

[1] Sometimes also called Navarro-Labourdin or Labourdin.

Proceedings of EMNLP 2011, Conference on Empirical Methods in Natural Language Processing, pages 39–48,
Edinburgh, Scotland, UK, July 27–31, 2011.

others (Alegria et al., 2011). However, these tools do not work well in processing the different dialects of Basque where lexical items have a different orthographic representation owing to slight differences in phonology and morphology.

Here is a brief contrastive example of the kinds of differences found in the (a) Lapurdian dialect and standard Basque (b) parallel corpus:[2]

(a) Ez gero uste izan **nexkatxa guziek** tu egiten **dautatela**
(b) Ez gero uste izan **neskatxa guztiek** tu egiten **didatela**

As the example illustrates, the differences are minor overall—the word order and syntax are unaffected, and only a few lexical items differ. This reflects the makeup of our parallel corpus quite well—in it, slightly less than 20% of the word tokens are distinct. However, even such relatively small discrepancies cause great problems in the potential reuse of current tools designed for the standard forms only.

We have experimented with two approaches that attempt to improve on a simple baseline of memorizing word-pairs in the dialect and the standard. The first approach is based on work by Almeida et al. (2010) on contrasting orthography in Brazilian Portuguese and European Portuguese. In this approach differences between substrings in distinct word-pairs are memorized and these transformation patterns are then applied whenever novel words are encountered in the evaluation. To prevent overgeneration, the output of this learning process is later subject to a morphological filter where only actual standard-form outputs are retained. The second approach is an Inductive Logic Programming-style (ILP) (Muggleton and De Raedt, 1994) learning algorithm where phonological transformation rules are learned from word-pairs. The goal is to find a minimal set of transformation rules that is both necessary and sufficient to be compatible with the learning data, i.e. the word pairs seen in the training data.

The remainder of the paper is organized as follows. The characteristics of the corpus available to us are described in section 2. In sections 3, 4, and 5, we describe the steps and variations of the methods we have applied and how they are evaluated. Section 6 presents the experimental results, and finally, we discuss the results and present possibilities for potential future work in section 7.

[2]English translation of the example: *Don't think all girls spit on me*

1.1 Related work

The general problem of supervised learning of dialectal variants or morphological paradigms has been discussed in the literature with various connection to computational phonology, morphology, machine learning, and corpus-based work. For example, Kestemont et al. (2010) presents a language-independent system that can 'learn' intra-lemma spelling variation. The system is used to produce a consistent lemmatization of texts in Middle Dutch literature in a medieval corpus, Corpus-Gysseling, which contains manuscripts dated before 1300 AD. These texts have enormous spelling variation which makes a computational analysis difficult.

Koskenniemi (1991) provides a sketch of a discovery procedure for phonological two-level rules. The idea is to start from a limited number of paradigms (essentially pairs of input-output forms where the input is the surface form of a word and the output a lemmatization plus analysis). The problem of finding phonological rules to model morphological paradigms is essentially similar to the problem presented in this paper. An earlier paper, Johnson (1984), presents a 'discovery procedure' for learning phonological rules from data, something that can be seen as a precursor to the problem dealt with by our ILP algorithm.

Mann and Yarowsky (2001) present a method for inducing translation lexicons based on transduction models of cognate pairs via bridge languages. Bilingual lexicons within languages families are induced using probabilistic string edit distance models. Inspired by that paper, Scherrer (2007) uses a generate-and-filter approach quite similar to our first method. He compares different measures of graphemic similarity applied to the task of bilingual lexicon induction between Swiss German and Standard German. Stochastic transducers are trained with the EM algorithm and using handmade transduction rules. An improvement of 11% in F-score is reported over a baseline method using Levenshtein Distance.

	Full corpus	80% part.	20% part.
Sentences	2,117	1,694	423
Words	12,150	9,734	2,417
Unique words			
Standard Basque	3,553	3,080	1,192
Lapurdian	3,830	3,292	1,239
Filtered pairs	3,610	3,108	1,172
Identical pairs	2,532	2,200	871
Distinct pairs	1,078	908	301

Table 1: Characteristics of the parallel corpus used for experiments.

2 The corpus

The parallel corpus used in this research is part of "TSABL" project developed by the IKER group in Baiona (fr. Bayonne).[3] The researchers of the IKER project have provided us with examples of the Lapurdian dialect and their corresponding forms in standard Basque. Our parallel corpus then contains running text in two variants: complete sentences of the Lapurdian dialect and equivalent sentences in standard Basque.

The details of the corpus are presented in table 1. The corpus consists of 2,117 parallel sentences, totaling 12,150 words (roughly 3,600 types). In order to provide data for our learning algorithms and also to test their performance, we have divided the corpus into two parts: 80% of the corpus is used for the learning task (1,694 sentences) and the remaining 20% (423 sentences) for evaluation of the learning process. As is seen, roughly 23% of the word-pairs are distinct. Another measure of the average deviation between the word pairs in the corpus is given by aligning all word-pairs by minimum edit distance (MED): aligning the 3,108 word-pairs in the learning corpus can be done at a total MED cost of 1,571. That is, roughly every 14th character in the dialect data is different from the standard form.

3 The baseline

The baseline of our experiments is a simple method, based on a dictionary of equivalent words with the list of correspondences between words extracted from the learning portion (80%) of the corpus. This list of correspondences contains all different word pairs in the variant vs. standard corpus. The baseline approach consists simply of memorizing all the distinct word pairs seen between the dialectal and standard forms, and subsequently applying this knowledge during the evaluation task. That is, if an input word during the evaluation has been seen in the training data, we provide the corresponding previously known output word as the answer. Otherwise, we assume that the output word is identical to the input word.

4 Overview of methods

We have employed two different methods to produce an application that attempts to extract generalizations from the training corpus to ultimately be able to produce the equivalent standard word corresponding to a given dialectal input word. The first method is based on already existing work by Almeida et al. (2010) that extracts all substrings from lexical pairs that are different. From this knowledge we then produce a number of phonological replacement rules that model the differences between the input and output words. In the second method, we likewise produce a set of phonological replacement rules, using an ILP approach that directly induces the rules from the pairs of words in the training corpus.

The core difference between the two methods is that while both extract replacement patterns from the word-pairs, the first method does not consider negative evidence in formulating the replacement rules. Instead, the existing morphological analyzer is used as a filter after applying the rules to unknown text. The second method, however, uses negative evidence from the word-pairs in delineating the replacement rules as is standard in ILP-approaches, and the subsequent morphological filter for the output plays much less of a role. Evaluating and comparing both approaches is motivated because the first method may produce much higher recall by virtue of generating a large number of input-output candidates during application, and the question is whether the corresponding loss in precision may be mitigated by judicious application of post-processing filters.

[3] *Towards a Syntactic Atlas of the Basque Language*, web site: *http://www.iker.cnrs.fr/-tsabl-towards-a-syntactic-atlas-of-.html*

4.1 Format of rules

Both of the methods we have evaluated involve learning a set of string-transformation rules to convert words, morphemes, or individual letters (graphemes) in the dialectal forms to the standard variant. The rules that are learned are in the format of so-called phonological replacement rules (Beesley and Karttunen, 2002) which we have later converted into equivalent finite-state transducers using the freely available *foma* toolkit (Hulden, 2009a). The reason for the ultimate conversion of the rule set to finite-state transducers is twofold: first, the transducers are easy to apply rapidly to input data using available tools, and secondly, the transducers can further be modified and combined with the standard morphology already available to us as a finite transducer.

In its simplest form, a replacement rule is of the format

$$A \rightarrow B \mid\mid C \_ D \tag{1}$$

where the arguments A,B,C,D are all single symbols or strings. Such a rule dictates the transformation of a string A to B, whenever the A occurs between the strings C and D. Both C and D are optional arguments in such a rule, and there may be multiple conditioning environments for the same rule.

For example, the rule:

```
h -> 0 || p _ , t _ , l _ , _ a s o
```

(2)

would dictate a deletion of h in a number of contexts; when the h is preceded by a p, t, or l, or succeeded by the sequence *aso*, for instance transforming *ongiethorri* (Lapurdian) to *ongietorri* (Batua).

As we will be learning several rules that each target different input strings, we have a choice as to the mode of application of the rules in the evaluation phase. The learned rules could either be applied in some specific order (sequentially), or applied simultaneously without regard to order (in parallel).

For example, the rules:

```
u -> i || z a _        (3)
k -> g || z a u _      (4)
```

would together (in parallel) change *zaukun* into *zaigun*. Note that if we imposed some sort of ordering on the rules and the `u` → `i` rule in the set would apply first, for example, the conditioning environment for the second rule would no longer be met after transforming the word into *zaikun*. We have experimented with sequential as well as parallel processing, and the results are discussed below.

4.2 Method 1 (lexdiff) details

The first method is based on the idea of identifying sequences inside word pairs where the output differs from the input. This was done through the already available tool *lexdiff* which has been used in automatic migration of texts between different Portuguese orthographies (Almeida et al., 2010). The *lexdiff* program tries to identify sequences of changes from seen word pairs and outputs string correspondences such as, for example: `76 ait -> at ; 39 dautz -> diz` (stemming from pairs such as (*joaiten/joaten* and *dautzut/dizut*), indicating that `ait` has changed into `at` 76 times in the corpus, etc., thus directly providing suggestions as to phonologically regular changes between two texts, with frequency information included.

With such information about word pairs we generate a variety of replacement rules which are then compiled into finite transducers with the *foma* application. Even though the *lexdiff* program provides a direct string-to-string change in a format that is directly compilable into a phonological rule transducer, we have experimented with some possible variations of the specific type of phonological rule we want to output:

- We can restrict the rules by frequency and require that a certain type of change be seen at least n times in order to apply that rule. For example, if we set this threshold to 3, we will only apply a string-to-string changing rule that has been seen three or more times.

- We limit the number of rules that can be applied to the same word. Sometimes the *lexdiff* application divides the change between a pair of words into two separate rules. For example the word-word correspondence *agerkuntza/agerpena* is expressed by two rules: `rkun -> rpen` and `ntza -> na`. Now, given these two rules, we have to be able to apply both to produce the correct total change

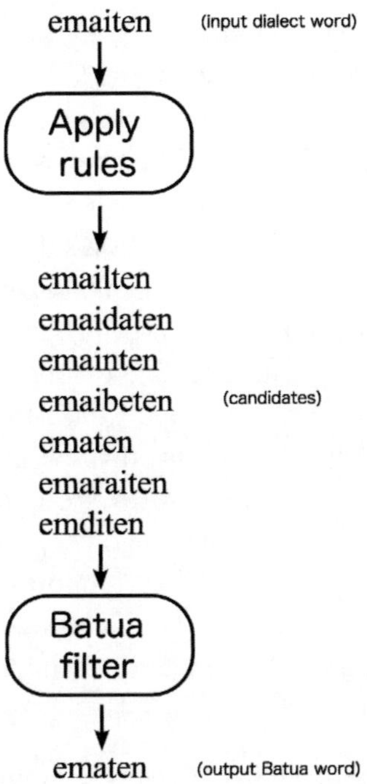

Figure 1: The role of the standard Basque (Batua) analyzer in filtering out unwanted output candidates created by the induced rule set produced by method 1.

agerkuntza/agerpena. By limiting the number of rules that can apply to a single input word we can avoid creating many spurious outputs, but also at the same time we may sacrifice some ability to produce the desired output forms.

- We can also control the application mode of the rules: sequential or parallel. If the previous two rules are applied in parallel, the form obtained from `agerkuntza` will not be correct since the *n* overlaps with the two rules. That is, when applying rules simultaneously in parallel, the input characters for two rules may not overlap. However, if these two rules applied in sequence (the order in this example is irrelevant), the output will be the correct: we first change `rkun -> rpen` and later `ntza -> na`. We have not a priori chosen to use parallel or sequential rules and have decided to evaluate both approaches.

- We can also compact the rules output by *lexdiff* by eliminating redundancies and constructing context-sensitive rules. For example: given a rule such as `rkun -> rpen`, we can convert this into a context-sensitive rule that only changes `ku` into `pe` when flanked by `r` and `n` to the left and right, respectively, i.e. producing a rule:

  `k u -> p e || r _ n` (5)

  This has a bearing on the previous point and will allow more rewritings within a single word in parallel replacement mode since there are fewer characters overlapping.

Once a set of rules is compiled with some instantiation of the various parameters discussed above and converted to a transducer, we modify the transducer in various ways to improve on the output.

First, since we already have access to a large-scale morphological transducer that models the standard Basque (Batua), we restrict the output from the conversion transducer to only allow those words as output that are legitimate words in standard Basque. Figure 1 illustrates this idea. In that figure, we see an input word in the dialect (*emaiten*) produce a number of candidates using the rules induced. However, after adding a morphological filter that models the Batua, we retain only one output.

Secondly, in the case that even after applying the Batua filter we retain multiple outputs, we simply choose the most frequent word (these unigram counts are gathered from a separate newspaper corpus of standard Basque).

4.3 Method 2 (ILP) details

The second method we have employed works directly from a collection of word-pairs (dialect/standard in this case). We have developed an algorithm that from a collection of such pairs seeks a minimal hypothesis in the form of a set of replacement rules that is consistent with all the changes found in the training data. This approach is generally in line with ILP-based machine learning methods (Muggleton and De Raedt, 1994). However, in contrast to the standard ILP, we do not learn statements of first-order logic that fit a collection of data, but rather, string-to-string replacement rules.[4]

[4]Phonological string-to-string replacement rules can be defined as collections of statements in first-order logic and compiled into transducers through such logical statements as well;

The two parameters to be induced are (1) the collection of string replacements $X \rightarrow Y$ needed to characterize the training data, and (2) the minimal conditioning environments for each rule, such that the collection of rules model the string transformations found in the training data.

The procedure employed for the learning task is as follows:

(1) Align all word pairs (using minimum edit distance by default).

(2) Extract a collection of phonological rewrite rules.

(3) For each rule, find counterexamples.

(4) For each rule, find the shortest conditioning environment such that the rule applies to all positive examples, and none of the negative examples. Restrict rule to be triggered only in this environment.

The following simple example should illustrate the method. Assuming we have a corpus of only two word pairs:

emaiten	ematen
igorri	igorri

in step (1) we would perform the alignment and produce the output

e	m	a	i	t	e	n	i	g	o	r	r	i
e	m	a	∅	t	e	n	i	g	o	r	r	i

From this data we would in step (2) gather that the only active phonological rule is $i \rightarrow \emptyset$, since all other symbols are unchanged in the data. However, we find two counterexamples to this rule (step 3), namely two i-symbols in *igorri* which do not alternate with ∅. The shortest conditioning environment that accurately models the data and produces no overgeneration (does not apply to any of the is in *igorri*) is therefore:

$$\texttt{i -> } \emptyset \ || \ \texttt{a \_} \quad (6)$$

see e.g. Hulden (2009b) for details. In other words, in this work, we skip the intermediate step of defining our observations as logical statements and directly convert our observations into phonological replacement rules.

the length of the conditioning environment being 1 (1 symbol needs to be seen to the left plus zero symbols to the right). Naturally, in this example we have two competing alternatives to the shortest generalization: we could also have chosen to condition the i-deletion rule by the t that follows the i. Both conditioning environments are exactly one symbol long. To resolve such cases, we a priori choose to favor conditioning environments that extend farther to the left. This is an arbitrary decision—albeit one that does have some support from phonology as most phonological assimilation rules are conditioned by previously heard segments—and very similar results are obtained regardless of left/right bias in the learning. Also, all the rules learned with this method are applied simultaneously (in parallel) in the evaluation phase.

4.3.1 String-to-string vs. single-symbol rules

In some cases several consecutive input symbols fail to correspond to the output in the learning data, as in for example the pairing

d	a	u	t
d	i	∅	t

corresponding to the dialect-standard pair *daut/dit*. Since there is no requirement in our formalism of rewrite rules that they be restricted to single-symbol rewrites only, there are two ways to handle this: either one can create a string-to-string rewriting rule:

au $\rightarrow i$ / CONTEXT

or create two separate rules

a $\rightarrow i$ / CONTEXT , u $\rightarrow \emptyset$ / CONTEXT

where CONTEXT refers to the minimal conditioning environment determined by the rest of the data. We have evaluated both choices, and there is no notable difference between them in the final results.

5 Evaluation

We have measured the quality of different approaches by the usual parameters of precision, recall and the harmonic combination of them, the F_1-score, and analyzed how the different options in the two approaches affect the results of these three parameters. Given that we, especially in method 1, extract quite a large number of rules and that each input word generates a very large number of candidates if we use all the rules extracted, it is possible to produce a high recall on the conversion of unknown dialect words to the standard form. However, the downside is that this naturally leads to low precision as well, which we try to control by introducing a number of filters to remove some of the candidates output by the rules. As mentioned above, we use two filters: (1) an obligatory filter which removes all candidate words that are not found in the standard Basque (by using an existing standard Basque morphological analyzer), and (2) using an optional filter which, given several candidates in the standard Basque, picks the most frequently occurring one by a unigram count from the separate newspaper corpus. This latter filter turns out to serve a much more prominent role in improving the results of method 1, while it is almost completely negligible for method 2.

6 Results

As mentioned above, the learning process has made use of 80% of the corpus, leaving 20% of the corpus for evaluation of the above-mentioned approaches. In the evaluation, we have only tested those words in the dialect that *differ* from words in the standard (which are in the minority). In total, in the evaluation part, we have tested the 301 words that differ between the dialect and the standard in the evaluation part of the corpus.

The results for the baseline—i.e. simple memorization of word-word correspondences—are (in %): P = 95.62, R = 43.52 and F_1 = 59.82. As expected, the precision of the baseline is high: when the method gives an answer it is usually the correct one. But the recall of the baseline is low, as is expected: slightly less than half the words in the evaluation corpus have been encountered before.[5]

6.1 Results with the lexdiff method

Table 2 shows the initial experiment of method 1 with different variations on the frequency

	P	**R**	**F_1**
$f \geq 1$	38.95	66.78	49.20
$f \geq 2$	46.99	57.14	51.57
$f \geq 3$	49.39	53.82	51.51

Table 2: Values obtained for Precision, Recall and F-scores with method 1 by changing the minimum frequency of the correspondences to construct rules for *foma*. The rest of the options are the same in all three experiments: only one rule is applied within a word.

	P	**R**	**F_1**
$f \geq 1$	70.28	58.13	63.64
$f \geq 2$	70.18	53.16	60.49
$f \geq 3$	71.76	51.50	59.96

Table 3: Values obtained for Precision, Recall and F-score with method 1 by changing the threshold frequency of the correspondences and applying a post-filter.

threshold—this is the limit on the number of times we must see a string-change to learn it. The results clearly show that the more examples we extract (frequency 1), the better results we obtain for recall while at the same time the precision suffers since many spurious outputs are given—even many different ones that each legitimately correspond to a word in the standard dialect. The F_1-score doesn't vary very much and it maintains similar values throughout. The problem with this approach is one which we have noted before: the rules produce a large number of outputs for any given input word and the consequence is that the precision suffers, even though only those output words are retained that correspond to actual standard Basque.

With the additional unigram filter in place, the results improve markedly. The unigram-filtered results are given in table 3.

We have also varied the maximum number of possible rule applications within a single word as well as applying the rules in parallel or sequentially, and compacting the rules to provide more context-sensitivity. We shall here limit ourselves to presenting the best results of all these options in terms of the F_1-score in table 4.

In general, we may note that applying more than

[5]The reason the baseline does not show 100% precision is that the corpus contains minor inconsistencies or accepted alternative spellings, and our method of measuring the precision suffers from such examples by providing both learned alternatives to a dialectal word, while only one is counted as being correct.

	P	R	F_1
Exp1	72.20	57.81	64.21
Exp2	72.13	58.47	64.59
Exp3	75.10	60.13	66.79

Table 4: Method 1. **Exp1**: frequency 2; 2 rules applied; in parallel; without contextual conditioning. **Exp2**: frequency 1; 1 rule applied; with contextual conditioning. **Exp3**: frequency 2; 2 rules applied; in parallel; with contextual conditioning.

one rule within a word has a negative effect on the precision while not substantially improving the recall. Applying the unigram filter—choosing the most frequent candidate—yields a significant improvement: much better precision but also slightly worse recall. Choosing either parallel or sequential application of rules (when more than one rule is applied to a word) does not change the results significantly. Finally, compacting the rules and producing context-sensitive ones is clearly the best option.

In all cases the F_1-score improves if the unigram filter is applied; sometimes significantly and sometimes only slightly. All the results of the table 4 which lists the best performing ones come from experiments where the unigram filter was applied.

Figure 2 shows how precision and recall values change in some of the experiments done with method 1. There are two different groups of points depending on if the unigram filter is applied, illustrating the tradeoff in precision and recall.

6.2 Results with the ILP method

The ILP-based results are clearly better overall, and it appears that the gain in recall by using method 1 does not produce F_1-scores above those produced with the ILP-method, irrespective of the frequency filters applied. Crucially, the negative evidence and subsequent narrowness of the replacement rules learned with the ILP method is responsible for the higher accuracy. Also, the results from the ILP-based method rely very little on the post-processing filters, as will be seen.

The only variable parameter with the ILP method concerns how many times a word-pair must be seen to be used as learning evidence for creating a replacement rule. As expected, the strongest result

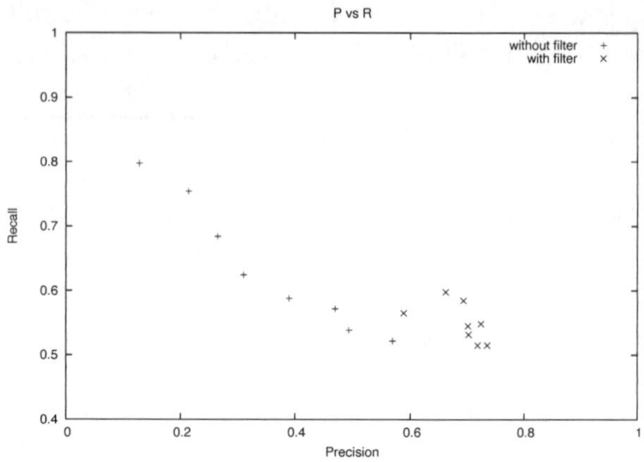

Figure 2: Tradeoffs of precision and recall values in the experiments with method 1 using various different parameters. When the unigram filter is applied the precision is much better, but the recall drops.

	P	R	F_1
$n = 1$	85.02 (86.13)	58.47 (57.80)	69.29 (69.18)
$n = 2$	82.33 (83.42)	54.15 (53.49)	65.33 (65.18)
$n = 3$	80.53 (82.07)	50.83 (50.17)	62.32 (62.26)
$n = 4$	81.19 (82.32)	50.17 (49.50)	62.01 (61.83)

Table 5: Experiments with the ILP method using a threshold of 1–4 (times a word-pair is seen) to trigger rule learning. The figures in parentheses are the same results with the added postprocessing unigram filter that, given several output candidates of the standard dialect, chooses the most frequent one.

is obtained by using all word-pairs, i.e. setting the threshold to 1. Table 5 shows the degradation of performance resulting from using higher thresholds.

Interestingly, adding the unigram filter that improved results markedly in method 1 to the output of the ILP method slightly worsens the results in most cases, and gives no discernible advantage in others. In other words, in those cases where the method provides multiple outputs, choosing the most frequent one on a unigram frequency basis gives no improvement over not doing so.

Additionally, there is comparatively little advantage with this method in adding the morphological filter to the output of the words in method 2 (this is the filter that rules out non-standard words). The results in table 5 include the morphological filter, but omitting it altogether brings down the best F_1

	P	R	F_1
Baseline	95.62	43.52	59.82
Method 1 (lexdiff)	75.10	60.13	66.79
Method 2 (ILP)	85.02	58.47	69.29

Table 6: The best results (per F_1-score of the two methods). The parameters of method 1 included using only those string transformations that occur at least 2 times in the training data, and limiting rule application to a maximum of 2 times within a word, and including a unigram post-filter. Rules were contextually conditioned. For method 2, all the examples (threshold 1) in the training data were used as positive and negative evidence, without a unigram filter.

to 56.14 from 69.29. By contrast, method 1 depends heavily on it and omitting the filter brings down the F_1-score from 66.79 to 11.53 with the otherwise strongest result of method 1 seen in table 6. The most prominent difference between the two approaches is that while method 1 can be finetuned using frequency information and various filters to yield results close to method 2, the ILP approach provides equally robust results without any additional information—in particular, frequency information of the target language. We also find a much lower rate of errors of commission with the ILP method; this is somewhat obvious as it takes advantage of negative evidence directly while the first method only does so indirectly through filters added later.

7 Conclusions and future work

We have presented a number of experiments to solve a very concrete task: given a word in the Lapurdian dialect of Basque, produce the equivalent standard Basque word. As background knowledge, we have a complete standard Basque morphological analyzer and a small parallel corpus of dialect and standard text. The approach has been based on the idea of extracting string-to-string transformation rules from the parallel corpus, and applying these rules to unseen words. We have been able to improve on the results of a naive baseline using two methods to infer phonological rules of the information extracted from the corpus and applying them with finite state transducers. In particular, the second method, inferring minimal phonological rewrite rules using an Inductive Logic Programming-style approach, seems promising as regards inferring phonological and morphological differences that are quite regular in nature between the two language variants. We expect that a larger parallel corpus in conjunction with this method could potentially improve the results substantially—with a larger set of data, thresholds could be set so that morphophonological generalizations are triggered only after a sufficient number of training examples (avoiding overgeneration), and, naturally, many more unique, non-regular, lexical correspondences could be learned.

During the current work, we have also accumulated a small but valuable training and test corpus which may serve as a future resource for evaluation of phonological and morphological rule induction algorithms.

In order to improve the results, we plan to research the combination of the previous methods with other ones which infer dialectal paradigms and relations between lemmas and morphemes for the dialect and the standard. These inferred relations could be contrasted with the information of a larger corpus of the dialect without using an additional parallel corpus.

Acknowledgments

We are grateful for the insightful comments provided by the anonymous reviewers. This research has been partially funded by the Spanish Science and Innovation Ministry via the OpenMT2 project (TIN2009-14675-C03-01) and the European Commission's 7th Framework Program under grant agreement no. 238405 (CLARA).

References

Alegria, I., Aranzabe, M., Arregi, X., Artola, X., Díaz de Ilarraza, A., Mayor, A., and Sarasola, K. (2011). Valuable language resources and applications supporting the use of Basque. In Vetulani, Z., editor, *Lecture Notes in Artifitial Intelligence*, volume 6562, pages 327–338. Springer.

Alegria, I., Aranzabe, M., Ezeiza, N., Ezeiza, A., and Urizar, R. (2002). Using finite state technology in natural language processing of basque.

In *LNCS: Implementation and Application of Automata*, volume 2494, pages 1–12. Springer.

Almeida, J. J., Santos, A., and Simoes, A. (2010). Bigorna–a toolkit for orthography migration challenges. In *Seventh International Conference on Language Resources and Evaluation (LREC2010), Valletta, Malta.*

Beesley, K. R. and Karttunen, L. (2002). Finite-state morphology: Xerox tools and techniques. *Studies in Natural Language Processing. Cambridge University Press.*

Hulden, M. (2009a). Foma: a finite-state compiler and library. In *Proceedings of the 12th Conference of the European Chapter of the Association for Computational Linguistics: Demonstrations Session*, pages 29–32, Athens, Greece. Association for Computational Linguistics.

Hulden, M. (2009b). Regular expressions and predicate logic in finite-state language processing. In Piskorski, J., Watson, B., and Yli-Jyrä, A., editors, *Finite-State Methods and Natural Language Processing—Post-proceedings of the 7th International Workshop FSMNLP 2008*, volume 191 of *Frontiers in Artificial Intelligence and Applications*, pages 82–97. IOS Press.

Johnson, M. (1984). A discovery procedure for certain phonological rules. In *Proceedings of the 10th international conference on Computational linguistics*, COLING '84, pages 344–347. Association for Computational Linguistics.

Kestemont, M., Daelemans, W., and Pauw, G. D. (2010). Weigh your words—memory-based lemmatization for Middle Dutch. *Literary and Linguistic Computing*, 25(3):287–301.

Koskenniemi, K. (1991). A discovery procedure for two-level phonology. *Computational Lexicology and Lexicography: A Special Issue Dedicated to Bernard Quemada*, pages 451–446.

Mann, G. S. and Yarowsky, D. (2001). Multipath translation lexicon induction via bridge languages. In *Proceedings of the second meeting of the North American Chapter of the Association for Computational Linguistics on Language technologies*, NAACL '01, pages 1–8.

Muggleton, S. and De Raedt, L. (1994). Inductive Logic Programming: theory and methods. *The Journal of Logic Programming*, 19:629–679.

Scherrer, Y. (2007). Adaptive string distance measures for bilingual dialect lexicon induction. In *Proceedings of the 45th Annual Meeting of the ACL: Student Research Workshop*, ACL '07, pages 55–60. Association for Computational Linguistics.

Modeling of Stylistic Variation in Social Media with Stretchy Patterns

Philip Gianfortoni
Carnegie Mellon University
Language Technologies Institute
Pittsburgh, PA
pwg@cs.cmu.edu

David Adamson
Carnegie Mellon University
Language Technologies Institute
Pittsburgh, PA
dadamson@cs.cmu.edu

Carolyn P. Rosé
Carnegie Mellon University
Language Technologies Institute
Pittsburgh, PA
cprose@cs.cmu.edu

Abstract

In this paper we describe a novel feature discovery technique that can be used to model stylistic variation in sociolects. While structural features offer much in terms of expressive power over simpler features used more frequently in machine learning approaches to modeling linguistic variation, they frequently come at an excessive cost in terms of feature space size expansion. We propose a novel form of structural features referred to as "stretchy patterns" that strike a balance between expressive power and compactness in order to enable modeling stylistic variation with reasonably small datasets. As an example we focus on the problem of modeling variation related to gender in personal blogs. Our evaluation demonstrates a significant improvement over standard baselines.

1 Introduction

The contribution of this paper is a novel approach to feature induction seeking to model stylistic variation at a level that not only achieves high performance, but generalizes across domains better than alternative techniques. Building on an earlier template based approach for modeling sarcasm (Tsur et al., 2010), we investigate the use of what we have termed "stretchy" features to model stylistic variation related to sociolects, which can be thought of as a form of dialect. Specifically, we focus on the problem of gender based classification. Gender classification and age classification have both received increased attention in the social media analysis community in recent years (Goswami et al., 2009; Barbieri, 2008; Cieri et al., 2004), most likely because large data sets annotated with these variables have recently become available. Machine learning technology provides a lens with which to explore linguistic variation that complements earlier statistical techniques used by variationist sociolinguists in their work mapping out the space of dialect variation and its accompanying social interpretation (Labov, 2010a; Labov, 2010b; Eckert & Rickford, 2001). These complementary approaches share a common foundation in numerical methods, however while descriptive statistics and inferential statistics mainly serve the purpose of describing non-random differences in distributions between communities, machine learning work in the area of social media analysis asks the more challenging question of whether the differences described are big enough to enable identification of community membership by means of those differences.

In the remainder of the paper, we first introduce prior work in a variety of related areas that both demonstrates why generalizable models characterizing sociolects within social media contexts are challenging to create and motivates our novel approach. Next we describe our

Proceedings of EMNLP 2011, Conference on Empirical Methods in Natural Language Processing, pages 49–59,
Edinburgh, Scotland, UK, July 27–31, 2011.

technical approach for inducing "stretchy patterns". We then present a series of experiments that demonstrate that our stretchy patterns provide advantages over alternative feature spaces in terms of avoiding overfitting to irrelevant content-based features as evidenced both in terms of achieving higher performance with smaller amounts of training data and in terms of generalizing better across subpopulations that share other demographic and individual difference variables.

2 Prior Work

Analysis of social media has grown in popularity over the past decade. Nevertheless, results on problems such as gender classification (Argamon et al., 2003), age classification (Argamon et al., 2007), political affiliation classification (Jiang & Argamon, 2008), and sentiment analysis (Wiebe et al., 2004) demonstrate how difficult stylistic classification tasks can be, and even more so when the generality is evaluated by testing models trained in one domain on examples from another domain. Prior work on feature engineering has attempted to address this generalization difficulty. Here we motivate our "stretchy pattern" approach to feature engineering for modeling sociolects, using gender analysis as a lens through which to understand the problem.

2.1 Variation Analysis and Gender

Since the earliest work in the area of variationist sociolinguistics, gender has been a variable of interest, which explains interesting differences in communication style that have been the topic of discussion both in academic circles (Holmes & Meyerhoff, 2003) and in the popular press (Tannen, 2001). The immense significance that has been placed on these differences, whether they are viewed as essentially linked to inherent traits, learned cultural patterns, or socially situated identities that are constructed within interaction, warrants attention to gender based differences within the scope of dialect variation. While one may view gender differences in communication from multiple angles, including topic, stance, and style, we focus specifically on linguistic style in our work.

Numerous attempts to computationally model gender based language variation have been published in the past decade (Corney et al., 2002; Argamon et al., 2003; Schler et al., 2005; Schler, 2006; Yan & Yan, 2006; Zhang et al., 2009; Mukherjee & Liu, 2010). Gender based language variation arises from multiple sources. For example, within a single corpus comprised of samples of male and female language that the two genders do not speak or write about the same topics. This has been reported to be the case with blog corpora such as the one used in this paper. Even in cases where pains have been taken to control for the distribution of topics associated with each gender within a corpus (Argamon et al., 2003), it's still not clear the extent to which that distribution is completely controlled. For example, if one is careful to have equal numbers of writing samples related to politics from males and females, it may still be the case that males and females are discussing different political issues or are addressing political issues from a different role based angle. While these differences are interesting, they do not fit within the purview of linguistic style variation.

Word based features such as unigrams and bigrams are highly likely to pick up on differences in topic (Schler, 2006) and possibly perspective. Thus, in cases where linguistic style variation is specifically of interest, these features are not likely to be included in the set of features used to model the variation even if their use leads to high performance within restricted domains. Typical kinds of features that are used instead include part-of-speech (POS) n-grams (Koppel, 2002; Argamon et al., 2003), word structure features that cluster words according to endings that indicate part of speech (Zhang et al., 2009), features that indicate the distribution of word lengths within a corpus (Corney et al., 2002), usage of punctuation, and features related to usage of jargon (Schler et al., 2005). In Internet-based communication, additional features have been investigated such as usage of internet specific features including "internet speak" (e.g., lol, wtf, etc.), emoticons, and URLs (Yan & Yan, 2006). In addition to attention to feature space design issues, some work on computational modeling of gender based language variation has included the development of novel feature selection techniques, which have also had a significant impact on success (Mukherjee & Liu, 2010; Zhang, Dang, & Chen, 2009).

Of these features, the only ones that capture stylistic elements that extend beyond individual words at a time are the POS ngram features. The inclusion of these features has been motivated by their hypothesized generality, although in practice, the generality of gender prediction models has not been formally evaluated in the gender prediction literature.

2.2 Domain Adaptation in Social Media

Recent work in the area of domain adaptation (Arnold et al., 2008; Daumé III, 2007; Finkel & Manning, 2009) raises awareness of the difficulties with generality of trained models and offers insight into the reasons for the difficulty with generalization. We consider these issues specifically in connection with the problem of modeling gender based variation.

One problem, also noted by variationist sociolinguists, is that similar language variation is associated with different variables (McEnery, 2006). For example, linguistic features associated with older age are also more associated with male communication style than female communication style for people of the same age (Argamon et al., 2007). Another problem is that style is not exhibited by different words than those that serve the purpose of communicating content. Thus, there is much about style that is expressed in a topic specific way.

What exacerbates these problems in text processing approaches is that texts are typically represented with features that are at the wrong level of granularity for what is being modeled. Specifically, for practical reasons, the most common types of features used in text classification tasks are still unigrams, bigrams, and part-of-speech bigrams. While relying heavily on these relatively simple features has computational advantages in terms of keeping the feature space size manageable, which aids in efficient model learning, in combination with the complicating factors just mentioned, these text classification approaches are highly prone to over-fitting.

Specifically, when text is represented with features that operate at too fine grained of a level, features that truly model the target style are not present within the model. Thus, the trained models are not able to capture the style itself and instead capture features that merely correlate with that style within the data. Thus, in cases where the data is not independent and identically distributed (IID), and where instances that belong to different subpopulations within the non-IID data have different class value distributions, the model will tend to give weight to features that indicate the subpopulation rather than features that model the style. This may lead to models that perform well within datasets that contain the same distribution of subpopulations, but will not generalize to different subpopulations, or even datasets composed of different proportions of the same subpopulations. Models employing primarly unigrams and bigrams as features are particularly problematic in this respect.

2.3 Automatic Feature Engineering

In recent years, a variety of manual and automatic feature engineering techniques have been developed in order to construct feature spaces that are adept at capturing interesting language variation without overfitting to content based variation, with the hope of leading to more generalizable models.

POS n-grams, which have frequently been utilized in genre analysis models (Argamon et al., 2003), are a strategic balance between informativity and simplicity. They are able to estimate syntactic structure and style without modeling it directly. In an attempt to capture syntactic structure more faithfully, there has been experimentation within the area of sentiment analysis on using syntactic dependency features (Joshi & Rosé, 2009; Arora, Joshi, & Rosé, 2009). However, results have been mixed. In practice, the added richness of the features comes at a tremendous cost in terms of dramatic increases in feature space size. What has been more successful in practice is templatizing the dependency features in order to capture the same amount of structure without creating features that are so specific.

Syntactic dependency based features are able to capture more structure than POS bigrams, however, they are still limited to representing relationships between pairs of words within a text. Thus, they still leave much to be desired in terms of representation power. Experimentation with graph mining from dependency parses has also been used for generating rich feature spaces (Arora et al., 2010). However, results with these features has also been disappointing. In practice, the rich features with real predictive power end up being difficult to find amidst myriads of useless features that simply add noise to the model. One direction that has proven successful at exceeding the representational power and performance of POS bigrams with only a very modest increase in feature space size has been a genetic programming based approach to learning to build a strategic set of rich features so that the benefits of rich features can be obtained without the expense in terms of feature space expansion. Successful experiments with this technique have been conducted in the area of sentiment analysis, with terminal symbols including unigrams in one case (Mayfield & Rosé, 2010) and graph features extracted from dependency parses in another (Arora et al., 2010). Nevertheless, improvements using these strategic sets of evolved features have been very small even where statistically significant, and thus it is difficult to justify adding so much machinery for such a small improvement.

Another direction is to construct template based features that combine some aspects of POS n-grams in that they are a flat representation, and the backoff version of dependency features, in that the symbols represent sets of words, which may be POS tags, learned word classes, distribution based word classes (such as high frequency words or low frequency words), or words. Such types of features have been used alone or in combination with sophisticated feature selection techniques or bootstrapping techniques, and have been applied to problems such as detection of sarcasm (Tsur et al., 2010), detection of causal connections between events (Girju, 2010), or machine translation (Gimpel et al., 2011). Our work is most similar to this class of approaches.

3 Technical Approach: Stretchy Patterns

Other systems have managed to extract and employ patterns containing gaps with some success. For example, Gimpel (2011) uses Gibbs sampling to collect patterns containing single-word gaps, and uses them among other features in a machine translation system.

Our patterns are more like the ones described in Tsur (2010), which were applied to the task of identifying sarcasm in sentences. We predicted that a similar method would show promise in extracting broader stylistic features indicative of the author's group-aligned dialect. We have chosen the classification of an author's gender as the task to which we can apply our patterns.

3.1 Pattern-Based Features

To extract their sarcasm-detecting patterns, Tsur (2010) first defined two sets of words: High Frequency Words (HFW) and Content Words (CW). The HFW set contained all words that occurred more than 100 times per million, and the CW set contained all words in the corpus that occurred fewer than 1000 times per million. Thus, a word could be contained in the HFW set, the CW set, or both. Such patterns must begin and end with words in the HFW set, and (as in our implementation) are constrained in the number of words drawn from each set. Additionally, as a preprocessing step, in their approach they made an attempt to replace phrases belonging to several categories of domain-specific phrases, such as product and manufacturer names with a label string, which was then added to the HFW set, indicating membership. For example, given an input such as "Garmin apparently does not care much about product quality or customer support", a number of patterns would be produced, including "[company] CW does not CW much".

3.2 Stretchy Patterns

Tsur's patterns were applied as features to classify sentences as sarcastic (or not), within the domain of online product reviews. Here our implementation and application diverge from Tsur's — the blog corpus features large multi-sentence documents, and span a diverse set of topics and authors. We aim to use these patterns not to classify sentiment or subtlety, but to capture the style and structure employed by subsets of the author-population.

We define a document as an ordered list of tokens. Each token is composed of a surface-form lexeme and any additional syntactic or semantic information about the word at this position (in our case this is simply the POS tag, but other layers such as Named Entity might be included). We refer to any of the available forms of a token as a *type*. A category is a set of word-types. Each type must belong to at least one category. All categories have a corresponding label, by which they'll be referred to within the patterns to come. *Gap* is a special category, containing all types that aren't part of any other category. The types belonging to any defined category may also be explicitly added to the Gap category.

A *stretchy pattern* is defined as a sequence of categories, which must not begin or end with a Gap category. We designate any number of adjacent Gap instances in a pattern by the string "GAP+"[1] and every other category instance by its label. As a convention, the label of a singleton category is the name of the type contained in the category (thus "writes" would be the label of a category containing only surface form "writes" and "VBZ" would be the label of the a category containing only the POS tag "VBZ"). The overall number of Gap and non-Gap category instances comprising a pattern is restricted - following Tsur (2010), we allow no more than six tokens of either category. In the case of Gap instances, this restriction is placed on the number of underlying tokens, and not the collapsed GAP+ form.

A sequence of tokens in a document matches a pattern if there is some expansion where each token corresponds in order to the pattern's categories. A given instance of GAP+ will match between zero and six tokens, provided the total number of Gap instances in the pattern do not exceed six[2].

By way of example, two patterns follow, with two strings that match each. Tokens that match as Gaps are shown in parenthesis.

[*cc*] (GAP+) [*adj*] [*adj*]
"*and* (some clients were) *kinda popular*..."
"*from* (our) *own general* election..."

for (GAP+) [*third-pron*] (GAP+) [*end*] [*first-pron*]
"ready *for* () *them* (to end) . *I* am..."
"*for* (murdering) *his* (prose) . *i* want..."

Although the matched sequences vary in length and content, the stretchy patterns preserve information about the proximity and ordering of particular words and categories. They focus on the relationship between key (non-Gap) words, and allow a wide array of sequences to be matched by a single pattern in a way that traditional word-class n-grams would not.

Our "stretchy pattern" formalism strictly subsumes Tsur's approach in terms of representational power. In particular, we could generate the same patterns described in Tsur (2010) by creating a singleton surface form category for each word in Tsur's HFW and then creating a category called [CW] that contains all of the words in the Tsur CW set, in addition to the domain-specific product/manufacturer categories Tsur employed.

Label	Category Members
adj	JJ, JJR, JJS
cc	CC, IN
md	MD
end	<period>, <comma>, <question>, <exclamation>
first-pron	I, me, my, mine, im, I'm
second-pron	you, your, youre, you're, yours, y'all
third-pron	he, him
emotional	feel, hurt, lonely, love
time	hour, hours, late, min, minute, minutes, months, schedule, seconds, time, years,
male_curse	fucking, fuck, jesus, cunt, fucker
female_curse	god, bloody, pig, hell, bitch, pissed, assed, shit

Table 1. Word Categories

3.3 Word Categories

With the aim of capturing general usage patterns, and motivated by the results of corpus linguists and discourse analysts, a handful token categories were defined, after the fashion of the LIWC categories as discussed in Gill (2009). Tokens belonging to categories may be replaced with their category label as patterns are extracted from each document. As a token might belong to multiple categories, the same token sequence may generate, and therefore match multiple patterns.

Words from a list of 800 common prepositions, conjunctions, adjectives, and adverbs were included as singleton surface-form categories. Determiners in particular are absent from this list (and from the POS categories that follow), as their absence or presence in a noun phrase is one of the primary variations the stretchy gaps of our patterns were intended to smooth over.

A handful of POS categories were selected, reflecting previous research and predictions about gender differences in language usage. For example, to capture the "hedging" discussed in Holmes (2003) as more common in female speech, the modal tag MD was included as a singleton

1 *This is actually an extractor parameter, but we collapse all adjacent gaps for all our experiments.*

2 *The restrictions on gaps are extractor parameters, but we picked zero to six gaps for our experiments.*

category. A category comprising the coordinating conjunction and preposition tags (CC, IN) was included to highlight transitions in complicated or nested multi-part sentences.

Additionally, where previous results suggested variation within a category based on gender (e.g. swearing, as in McEnery (2006)), two categories were added, with the words most discriminative for each gender. However, even those words most favored by male authors might appear in contexts where males would never use them - it is our hope that by embedding these otherwise-distinguishing features within the structure afforded by gap patterns we can extract more meaningful patterns that more accurately and expressively capture the style of each gender.

3.4 Extraction and Filtering

Patterns are extracted from the training set, using a sliding window over the token stream to generate all allowable combinations of category-gap sequences within the window. This generates an exponential number of patterns - we initially filter this huge set based on each pattern's accuracy and coverage as a standalone classifier, discarding those with less than a minimum precision or number of instances within the training set. In the experiments that follow, these thresholds were set to a minimum of 60% per-feature precision, and at least 15 document-level hits.

4 Evaluation

We have motivated the design of our stretchy patterns by the desire to balance expressive power and compactness. The evidence of our success should be demonstrated along two dimensions: first, that these compact features allow our models to achieve a higher performance when trained on small datasets and second, that models trained with our stretchy patterns generalize better between domains. Thus, in this section, we present two evaluations of our approach in comparison to three baseline approaches.

4.1 Dataset

We chose to use the Blog Authorship Corpus for our evaluation, which has been used in earlier work related to gender classification (Schler 2006), and which is available for web download[3]. Each instance contains a series of personal blog entries from a single author. For each blog, we have metadata indicating the gender, age, occupation, and astrological sign of the author. From this corpus, for each experiment, we randomly selected a subset in which we have balanced the distribution of gender and occupation. In particular, we selected 10 of the most common occupations in the dataset, specifically Science, Law, Non-Profit, Internet, Engineering, Media, Arts, Education, Technology, and Student. We randomly select the same number of blogs from each of these occupations, and within occupation based sets, we maintain an even distribution of male and female authors. We treat the occupation variable as a proxy for topic since bloggers typically make reference to their work in their posts. We make use of this proxy for topic in our evaluation of domain generality below.

4.2 Baseline Approaches

We can find in the literature a variety of approaches to modeling gender based linguistic variation, as outlined in our prior work discussion above. If our purpose was to demonstrate that our stretchy patterns beat the state-of-the-art at the predictive task of gender classification, it would be essential to implement one of these approaches as our baseline. However, our purpose here is instead to address two more specific research questions instead, and for that we argue that we can learn something from comparing with three more simplistic baselines, which differ only in terms of feature extraction. The three baseline models we tested included a unigram model, a unigram+bigram model, and a Part-of-Speech bigram model. For part-of-speech tagging we used the Stanford part-of-speech tagger[4] (Toutanova et al., 2003).

Our three baseline feature spaces have been very commonly used in the language technologies community for a variety of social media analysis tasks, the most common of which in recent years has been sentiment analysis. While these feature spaces are simple, they have remained surprisingly strong baseline approaches when testing is done

3 http://u.cs.biu.ac.il/~koppel/BlogCorpus.htm

4 http://nlp.stanford.edu/software/tagger.shtml

within domain, and with large enough training sets. However, these relatively weak, low level features are notorious for low performance when datasets are too small and for low generalizability when evaluated in a cross-domain setting. Because of this, we expect to see our baseline approaches perform well when both training and testing data match in terms of topic distribution and when we use our largest amount of training data. However, we expect performance to degrade as training data set size decreases as well as when we test in a cross-domain setting. We expect to see degradation also with our proposed stretchy patterns. However, we will consider our claims to have been supported if we see less degradation with our stretchy patterns than with the baseline approaches.

We did minimal preprocessing on the textual data prior to feature extraction for all approaches. Specifically, all numbers in the text were replaced with a <number> symbol. Punctuation was separated from words and treated as a separate symbol. All tokens were downcased so that we generalize across capitalization options. In all cases, we use a support vector machine approach to training the model, using the SMO implementation found in Weka (Witten & Frank, 2005), using a linear polynomial kernel and default settings. For each model, we first use a Chi-Squared filter for attribute selection over the training data, retaining only the top 3,000 features prior to training.

4.3 Study 1: Learning on Small Datasets

The purpose of Study 1 was to test the claim that our stretchy patterns achieve higher performance when we train using a small amount of data. For this evaluation, we constructed a test set of 3,000 instances that we use consistently across training configurations. Specifically, we selected 300 blogs from each of the 10 occupations listed above such that 150 of them were from male authors and 150 from female authors. We constructed also a set of training sets of size 300, 800, 1500, 2000, and 3000 randomly selected blogs respectively, in which we maintain the same occupation and gender distribution as in the test set. To compensate for sampling eccentricities, two samples of each training size were extracted, and their results averaged for each experiment. In all cases, from each blog, we randomly selected one blog entry that was at least 100 words long. For each baseline approach as well as the stretchy feature approach, we build a model using each training set, which we then test using the common test set. Thus, for each approach, we can examine how performance increases as amount of training data increases, and we can compare this growth curve between approaches.

Training Set Size	Unigram	Unigram + Bigram	POS Bigram	Stretchy Patterns
300	49.9 (-.002)	49.85(-.002)	51.6 (.032)	48.65(-.027)
800	51.65(.029)	50.15 (.003)	50.55 (.014)	53.15 (.072)
1500	48.6 (-.028)	49.98 (0)	48.63 (-.028)	**53.95 (.066)**
2000	50.55(.011)	51.7 (.034)	51.82 (.063)	**53.98 (.079)**
3000	49.48(-.010)	50.8 (.016)	49.88 (.0025)	**59.05 (.181)**

Table 2 Classification accuracy for varying data sizes (with kappa in parentheses)

The dramatic mediocrity of the baselines' performance highlights the difficulty of the selected data set, confirming the sense that most of what these n-gram models pick up is not truly gender-specific usage, but shadows of the distribution of topics (here, occupations) between the genders. At all sizes except the smallest (where no approach is significantly better than random), our approach outperforms the baselines. At size 800, this difference is marginal ($p < .1$), and at the larger sizes, it is a significant increase ($p < .05$).

4.4 Study 2: Evaluation of Domain Generality

For our evaluation of domain generality, we randomly selected 200 blogs from each of the 10 most common occupations in the corpus, 100 of which were by male authors and 100 by female authors. As in the evaluation above, from each blog, we randomly selected one blog entry that was at least 100 words long. In order to test domain generality, we perform a leave-one-occupation-out cross validation experiment, which we refer to as a Cross Domain evaluation setting. In this setting, on each fold, we always test on blogs from an occupation that was not represented within the training data. Thus, indicators of gender that are specific to an occupation will not generalize from training to test.

Table 3 displays the results from the comparison of our stretchy feature approach with each of the baseline approaches. On average, stretchy patterns generalized better to new domains than the other approaches. The stretchy feature approach beat the baseline approaches in a statistically significant way ($p < .05$).

Occupation	Unigram	Unigram + Bigram	POS Bigram	Stretchy Patterns
Engineering	49.5 (-.01)	53 (.06)	49 (-.02)	50.5 (.01)
Education	49 (-.02)	52 (.04)	54.5 (.09)	51 (.02)
Internet	55.5 (.11)	47.5 (-.05)	55.5 (.11)	56.5 (.13)
Law	51.5 (.03)	46.5 (-.07)	46.5 (-.07)	50.5 (.01)
Non-Profit	50 (0)	54 (.08)	49 (-.02)	51. (.02)
Technology	50 (0)	53.5 (.07)	50 (0)	51.5 (.03)
Arts	48 (-.04)	46.5 (-.07)	51 (.02)	55.4 (.11)
Media	53 (.06)	50 (0)	45 (-.10)	51.5 (.02)
Science	52 (.04)	48 (-.04)	40.5 (-.19)	59.5 (.19)
Student	51 (.02)	46 (-.09)	55 (.10)	62 (.24)
Average	50.95 (.002)	49.7 (-.007)	49.6 (.01)	**53.94 (.08)**
Random CV	61.05 (.22)	59.65 (.19)	57.95 (.16)	**62.8 (.26)**

Table 3 Accuracy from leave-one-occupation-out cross-validation (with kappa in parentheses)

For random cross-validation, our approach performed marginally better than the unigram baseline, and again significantly exceeds the performance of the other two baselines. Note that for all approaches, there is a significant drop in performance from Random CV to the cross-domain setting, showing that all approaches, including ours, suffer from domain specificity to some extent. However, while all of the baselines drop down to essentially random performance in the cross-domain setting, and stretchy patterns remain significantly higher than random, we show that our approach has more domain generality, although it still leaves room for improvement on that score.

5 Qualitative Analysis of Results

Here we present a qualitative analysis of the sorts of patterns extracted by our method. Although we cannot draw broad conclusions from a qualitative investigation of such a small amount of data, we did observe some interesting trends.

As our features do not so much capture syntactic structure as the loose proximity and order of classes of words, we'll say less about structure and more about what sort of words show up in each others' neighborhood. In particular, a huge proportion of the top-ranked patterns feature instances of the [*end*] and [*first-pron*] categories, suggesting that much of the gender distinction captured by our patterns is to be found around sentence boundaries and self-references. It's believable and encouraging that "the way I talk about myself" is an important element in distinguishing style between genders.

The Chi-squared ranking of the stretchy patterns gives us a hint as to the predictive effect of each as a feature. In the discussion and examples that follow, we'll draw from the highest-ranked features, and refer to the weights' signs to label each pattern as "male" or "female".

In these features the discourse analyst or dialectician can find fodder for their favorite framework, or support for popularly held views on gender and language. For example, we find that about twice as many of the patterns containing either [*third-pron*] or [*second-pron*] in the neighborhood of [*first-pron*] are weighted toward female, supporting earlier findings that women are more concerned with considering interpersonal relationships in their discourse than are men, as in Kite (2002). For example,

> [*first-pron*] (GAP+) [*third-pron*]
> "*i* (have time for) *them*"

Supporting the notion that distinctively female language is "deviant," and viewed as a divergence from a male baseline, as discussed in Eckert & McConnell-Ginet (1992), we note that more of the top-ranked patterns are weighted toward female. This might suggest that the "female" style is less standard and therefore harder to detect. Additionally, we only find adjacent [*end*] markers, capturing repeated punctuation, in our female-weighted patterns. For instance,

> [*adj*] (GAP+) [*end*] (GAP+) [*end*] [*end*]
> "*new* (songs) *!* (:-) see yas) . ."

This divergence from the standard sentence form, while more common overall in informal electronic communications, does occur more frequently among female authors in the data. Further analysis of the data suggests that emoticons like *:-)* would have formed a useful category for our patterns, as they occur roughly twice as often in female posts, and often in the context of end-of-sentence punctuation.

We provide a rough numerical overview of the features extracted during the random cross-validation experiment. Samples of high-ranking stretchy patterns appear in Tables 4 and 5. Note that sequences may match more than one pattern, and that GAP+ expansions can have zero length.

[first-pron]
(female) and **i** have time for...
(female) a freshman , **my** brother is...
(male) and **i** overcame my fear ...

[*end*] (GAP+) [*first-pron*]
(female) no **! ! ! (i just guess) i**...
(female) all year **. (. .) i** am so...
(male) the internet **. () i** ask only...

[*end*] (GAP+) [*end*] and
(female) positives **. (gotta stay positive) . and** hey...
(female) at the park ..**(. sitting at teh bench alone ..). and** walking down on my memory line...
(male) sunflower **. (she has a few photo galleries ..). and** i would like...

***like* (GAP+) [*first-pron*]**
(female) well **like (anywho . . . I got) my** picture back...
(female) it's times **like (these that I miss) my** friends...
(male) with something **like (that in the air ,) i** don't...

Table 4. Female Patterns.

[*adj*] (GAP+) [*end*] (GAP+) [*first-pron*]
(male) her own **digital (camera) . (what enlightens) me** is...
(male) a **few (photo galleries ..) . (and) i** would...
(female) money **all (year) . (..) i** am so much...

[*first-pron*] (GAP+) [*end*]
(male) again . **i** (ate so well today , too) **.** lots of ...
(male) movie **i ('d already seen once before) .**
(female) a junior and **i (have the top locker) .** lol

[*end*] (GAP+) [*first-pron*] (GAP+) [*cc*]
(male) food **! () i ('m so hooked) on this delicious...**
(male) galleries **.(.. and) i (would like) for** you to...
(female) alot better **. () i (have a locker right) above**...

***so* (GAP+) [*end*]**
(male) was it ? **so (cousins , stay posted) .** remember...
(male) experience you've gained **so (far) .** if...
(female) , its been **so (damn crappy out) .** ok bye

Table 5. Male Patterns.

Although our patterns capture much more than the unigram frequencies of categories, a glance at such among the extracted patterns will prove enlightening. Of the 3000 patterns considered, 1407 were weighted to some degree toward male, and 1593 toward female. Overall, female patterns include more of our chosen categories than their male counterparts. Many of these imbalances matched our initial predictions, in particular the greater number of female patterns with [*first-pron*] (772 vs. 497), [*second-pron*] (47 vs 27), [*third-pron*] (286 vs. 203), and [*end*] (851 vs. 618), [emotion] (36 vs. 20).

Contrary to our expectations, [*md*] appeared only slightly more frequently in female patterns (73 vs. 66), and [*time*] appeared in only a few male patterns (22 female vs. 7 male) - of these time-patterns, most of the matching segments included the word "time" itself, instead of any other time-related words. No patterns containing the divided *curse* categories were among the top-ranked features.

6 Conclusions and Current Directions

In this paper we described a novel template based feature creation approach that we refer to as stretchy patterns. We have evaluated our approach two ways, once to show that with this approach we are able to achieve higher performance than baseline approaches when small amounts of training data are used, and one in which we demonstrated that we are able to achieve better performance in a cross domain evaluation setting.

While the results of our experiments have shown promising results, we acknowledge that we have scratched the surface of the problem we are investigating. First, our comparison was limited to just a couple of strategically selected baselines. However, there have been many variations in the literature on gender classification specifically, and genre analysis more generally, that we could have included in our evaluations, and that would likely offer additional insights. For example, we have tested our approach against POS bigrams, but we have not utilized longer POS sequences, which have been used in the literature on gender classification with mixed results. In practice, longer POS sequences have only been more valuable than POS bigrams when sophisticated feature selection techniques have been used (Mukherje & Liu, 2010). Attention may also be directed to the selection or generation of word categories better suited to stretchy patterns. Alternative approaches to selecting or clustering these features should also be explored.

7 Acknowledgements

This research was funded by ONR grant N000141110221 and NSF DRL-0835426.

References

Argamon, S., Koppel, M., Fine, J., & Shimoni, A. (2003). Gender, genre, and writing style in formal written texts, *Text*, 23(3), pp 321-346.

Argamon, S., Koppel, M., Pennebaker, J., & Schler, J. (2007). Mining the blogosphere: age, gender, and the varieties of self-expression. *First Monday* 12(9).

Arnold, A. (2009). Exploiting Domain And Task Regularities For Robust Named Entity Recognition. PhD thesis, Carnegie Mellon University, 2009.

Arora, S., Joshi, M., Rosé, C. P. (2009). Identifying Types of Claims in Online Customer Reviews, *Proceedings of the North American Chapter of the Association for Computational Linguistics*.

Arora, S., Mayfield, E., Rosé, C. P., & Nyberg, E. (2010). Sentiment Classification using Automatically Extracted Subgraph Features, *Proceedings of the NAACL HLT Workshop on Emotion in Text.*

Barbieri, F. (2008). Patterns of age-based linguistic variation in American English. *Journal of Sociolinguistics* 12(1), pp 58-88.

Cieri, C., Miller, D., & Walker, K. (2004). The fisher corpus: a resource for the next generations of speech-to-text. In *Proceedings of the 4th International Conference on Language Resources and Evaluation,* pp 69-71.

Corney, M., de Vel, O., Anderson, A., Mohay, G. (2002). Gender-preferential text mining of e-mail discourse, in the Proceedings of the 18th Annual Computer Security Applications Conference.

Daumé III, H. (2007). Frustratingly Easy Domain Adaptation. In Proceedings of the 45th Annual Meeting of the Association of Computational Linguistics, pages 256-263.

Eckert, P. & Rickford, J. (2001). *Style and Sociolinguistic Variation*, Cambridge: University of Cambridge Press.

Eckert, P. & McConnell-Ginet, S. (1992). Think Practically and Look Locally: Language and Gender as Community- Based Practice. In the *Annual Review of Anthropology,* Vol. 21, pages 461-490.

Finkel, J. & Manning, C. (2009). Hierarchical Bayesian Domain Adaptation. In *Proceedings of Human Language Technologies: The 2009 Annual Conference of the North American Chapter of the Association for Computational Linguistics*.

Gill, A., Nowson, S. & Oberlander, J. (2009). What Are They Blogging About? Personality, Topic and Motivation in Blogs. In *Proceedings of the Third International ICWSM Conference*.

Gimpel, K., Smith, N. A. (2011). Unsupervised Feature Induction for Modeling Long-Distance Dependencies in Machine Translation, *Forthcoming*.

Girju, R. (2010). Towards Social Causality: An Analysis of Interpersonal Relationships in Online Blogs and Forums, *Proceedings of the Fourth International AAAI Conference on Weblogs and Social Media*.

Goswami, S., Sarkar, S. & Rustagi, M. (2009). Stylometric analysis of bloggers' age and gender. In *Proceedings of the Third International ICWSM Conference*.

Holmes, J. & Meyerhoff, M. (2003). *The Handbook of Language and Gender*, Blackwell Publishing.

Jiang, M. & Argamon, S. (2008). Political leaning categorization by exploring subjectivities in political blogs. In *Proceedings of the 4th International Conference on Data Mining*, pages 647-653.

Joshi, M. & Rosé, C. P. (2009). Generalizing Dependency Features for Opinion Mining, *Proceedings of the Association for Computational Linguistics*.

Kite, M. (2002) Gender Stereotypes, in the *Encyclopedia of Women and Gender: Sex Similarities and DIfferences*, Volume 1, Academic Press.

Kristina Toutanova, Dan Klein, Christopher Manning, and Yoram Singer. 2003. Feature-Rich Part-of-Speech Tagging with a Cyclic Dependency Network. In *Proceedings of HLT-NAACL 2003*, pp. 252-259.

Labov, W. (2010a). *Principles of Linguistic Change: Internal Factors (Volume 1)*, Wiley-Blackwell.

Labov, W. (2010b). *Principles of Linguistic Change: Social Factors (Volume 2)*, Wiley-Blackwell.

Mayfield, E. & Rosé, C. P. (2010). Using Feature Construction to Avoid Large Feature Spaces in Text Classification, in *Proceedings of the Genetic and Evolutionary Computation Conference*.

McEnery, T. (2006). *Swearing in English: Bad language, purity and power from 1586 to the present,* Routledge.

Mukherjee, A. & Liu, B. (2010). Improved Gender Classification of Blog Authors, Proceedings of EMNLP 2010.

Schler, J., Koppel, M., Argamon, S., Pennebaker, J. (2005). Effects of Age and Gender on Blogging, Proceedings of AAAI Spring Symposium on Computational Approaches for Analyzing Weblogs.

Schler, J. (2006). Effects of Age and Gender on Blogging. *Artificial Intelligence*, *86*, 82-84.

Tannen, D. (2001). *You Just Don't Understand: Women and Men in Conversation*, First Quill.

Tsur, O., Davidov, D., & Rappoport, A. (2010). ICWSM – A Great Catchy Name: Semi-Supervised Recognition of Sarcastic Sentences in Online Product Reviews, *Proceedings of the Fourth International AAAI Conference on Weblogs and Social Media*.

Wiebe, J., Bruce, R., Martin, M., Wilson, T., & Ball, M. (2004). Learning Subjective Language, *Computational Linguistics*, 30(3).

Witten, I. & Frank, E. (2005). *Data Mining: Practical Machine Learning Tools and Techniques*, second edition, Elsevier, San Francisco.

Yan, X., & Yan, L. (2006). Gender classification of weblog authors. *AAAI Spring Symposium Series Computational Approaches to Analyzing Weblogs* (p. 228–230).

Zhang, Y., Dang, Y., Chen, H. (2009). Gender Difference Analysis of Political Web Forums : An Experiment on International Islamic Women's Forum, Proceedings of the 2009 IEEE international conference on Intelligence and security informatics, pp 61-64.

Adapting Slovak ASR for native Germans speaking Slovak

Štefan Beňuš [1,2], Miloš Cerňak[1], Milan Rusko[1], Marián Trnka[1], Sachia Darjaa[1]
[1] Institute of Informatics, Slovak Academy of Sciences, Bratislava, Slovakia
[2] Constantine the Philosopher University, Nitra, Slovakia

sbenus@ukf.sk, {Milos.Cernak, Milan.Rusko, Marian.Trnka, Sachia.Darzagin}@savba.sk

Abstract

We explore variability involved in speech with a non-native accent. We first employ a combination of knowledge-based and data-driven approaches for the analysis of pronunciation variants between L1 (German) and target L2 (Slovak). Knowledge gained in this two-step process is then used in adapting acoustic models and the lexicon. We focus on modifications in the pronunciation dictionary and speech rate. Our results show that the recognition of German-accented Slovak is significantly improved with techniques modeling slow L2 speech, and that the adaptation of the pronunciation dictionary yields only insignificant gains.

1 Introduction

Automatic recognition of non-native accented speech represents a complex problem, especially since this type of variability becomes more common even in languages with a relatively small number of speakers due to globalization and increased mobility of people. The methods most commonly used for dealing with this type of speech variability include pronunciation modeling, acoustic modeling, or topological modeling (Oh, Yoon and Kim, 2007, Tomokiyo, 2000). This paper presents an approach that starts with an analysis of the pronunciation variability of nonnative speech taking into account most salient differences between L1 language (in our case German) and L2 target language (Slovak). Following this knowledge-base step, a semi-automatic data-driven approach analyzes the pronunciation variants on a subset of a training corpus is proposed. The knowledge gained in this two-step process is then used to adapt our state-of-the-art ASR system for Slovak in an effort to improve the baseline recognition of this system in German accented Slovak. We primarily experiment with adapting the pronunciation dictionary and speech rate. In short, we test the acoustic model and lexicon adaptation based on the analysis of pronunciation proximity between the German-accented and standard varieties of Slovak.

The paper is structured as follows. Section 2 describes the corpora used for testing and training. Section 3 discusses differences between Slovak and German pronunciation by analyzing the phonological systems of the two languages (3.1) and by analyzing the errors Germans make when speaking Slovak (3.2). Section 4 presents the setup and results of experiments in adapting our state-of-the-art ASR system for Slovak to German-accented pronunciation of Slovak focusing on speech rate manipulation and appending pronunciation dictionary. Section 5 discusses the findings and concludes the paper.

2 Description of the databases

Our testing corpus consists of Slovak sentences read by 18 native speakers of German. The sentences were selected or created to represent four types of variability: dialectological (100), foreign accent (100), phonetic richness and balance (300), and prosody (90). The first type was based on common differences among Slovak dialects, the second specially designed for problematic areas of native German speakers speaking Slovak.

Proceedings of EMNLP 2011, Conference on Empirical Methods in Natural Language Processing, pages 60–64,
Edinburgh, Scotland, UK, July 27–31, 2011.

Depending on the L2 proficiency level of the subjects, they were divided into two groups: Beginner – Intermediate (A1-B1), and Upper-intermediate – Advanced (B2-C2). The subjects were evenly distributed into these two groups with 9 speakers each. The first group read sentences for the dialectological and accent tests accompanied by 100 phonetically rich and balance sentences, and the second group read all 590 sentences. In total, the testing corpus represents 8010 sentences (9*300 + 9*590).

3 Features of Slovak with German accent

3.1 Knowledge-based approach

One of the most common ways of predicting differences between native (L1) and foreign-accented (L2) speech is to compare the sound systems of L1 and L2. Here we present a brief overview of most robust pronunciation differences between German and Slovak.

In terms of segmental inventories, Slovak does not have front rounded vowels and has only one front mid vowel quality while German has two. Also, both languages have phonemically distinct short and long vowels, but the length distinction in German robustly affects vowel quality (short vowels being lax and more centralized), while this tendency for Slovak is much less salient and a mid central schwa is missing in the Slovak inventory (Beňuš and Mády 2010). Additionally, a major difference comes from Slovak palatal consonants (stops, nasal, and lateral) that are missing in German. Finally, /r/ is an apical trill in Slovak in all positions while it commonly has uvular or vocalized qualities in German.

Many allophonic processes are different in the two languages. The most perceptually salient include the aspiration of voiceless stops and the glottalization of initial vowels in German and its absence in Slovak. German lacks a so called dark /l/ quality in syllable codas while most /l/s in Slovak have this quality. In terms of phonotactics, Slovak has a richer set of potential onset clusters than German. Additionally, Slovak syllabic nuclei might be formed by liquids (/l/, /r/) that also participate in lengthening alternations, which is not the case in German. While both languages have pervasive voicing assimilation and neutralization, voicing neutralization in obstruent coda consonants is slightly more salient in German than in Slovak.

Finally, most salient prosodic differences include a fixed left-most word stress in Slovak (cf. variable in German). Slovak in general also reduces the length and quality of unstressed vowels minimally, while in German, unstressed vowels tend to be shortened and centralized.

3.2 Analysis of accent sentences

In this section we test the theoretical predictions of pronunciation problems in Slovak with German accent stemming from interferences between L1 and L2 described in the previous section. We took a subset of our corpus, 100 accent sentences read by all 18 speakers and asked trained annotators to mark all perceptually salient markers of accented speech at the level of segments together with word stress differences. Different annotators (N=6) were given identical instructions and labeled different subsets of the data. A single expert then checked all annotations for mistakes and inconsistencies.

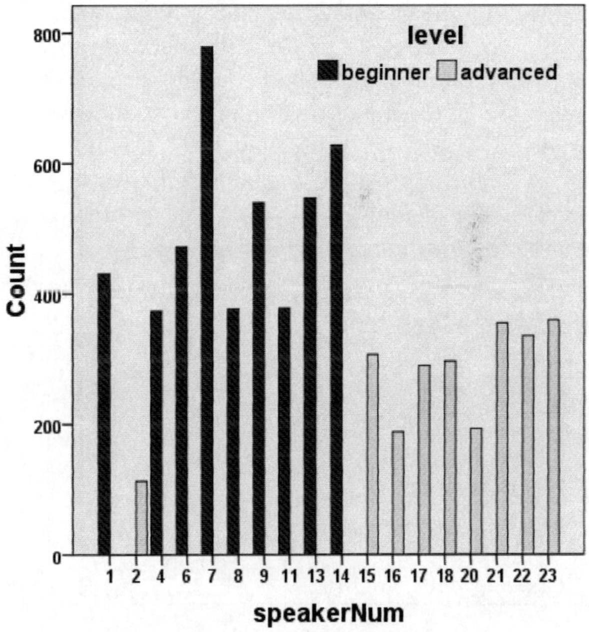

Figure 1. Error counts for all subjects divided by their L2 proficiency level (there were 2540 reference phonemes for each speaker)

The annotators found 6966 segmental differences between 'standard' and German accented Slovak, which represents 15.2% of all 45720 phonemes in the 1800 accent sentences. Roughly half of the differences involved syllable nuclei including liquids (53.1%) and the rest involved onset and coda consonants. The assignment to proficiency levels showed a fairly reasonable correspondence with the number of segmental problems in the accent sentences, as can be seen in Figure 1 above.

Given the discussion in Section 3.1, we noticed several expected and unexpected patterns in the distribution of pronunciation deviations. Table 1 below lists the most frequent groups of pronunciation problems. The expected problems involved differences in the palatalization of alveolar consonants (15.6%), and the presence of aspiration with voiceless plosives (3.3%). Two notable unexpected patterns were observed. First, despite some differences in the short and long syllabic nuclei, described in 3.1, the overall frequency of deviations in phonemic length was surprising: almost one third (31.6%) of all marked differences involved either the shortening of long nuclei or lengthening of short ones. Additionally, despite the clear and predictable placement of Slovak word stress, 13.7% of differences involved an incorrect placement of word stress. The production of German vowel quality (such as front rounded vowels or schwa) was relatively low (1.8%). Hence, prosodic and metrical features of vowels were perceived as far more problematic than the features related to their quality.

Type of error	Count	%
Vowel shortening	1164	16.7
Palatalization	1090	15.6
Obstruent voicing	1078	15.5
Vowel lengthening	1038	14.9
Nucleus stress	954	13.7
Rhotic	537	7.7
Aspiration	227	3.3
German vow. quality	123	1.8

Table 1: Most common errors in accent sentences

The second unexpected pattern was a relatively high frequency of differences in the voicing of obstruent consonants (15.5%). The majority of these cases included the devoicing of consonants that, in regular fluent Slovak, would be produced as voiced. This pattern is related to pervasive coda voicing neutralization in German mentioned in section 3.1. Voicing of canonically voiceless consonants was observed as well, especially in the voicing of /s/ to /z/.

It is worth noting that both of the unexpected patterns relate to speech rate. A generally slower rate of L2 speakers results in frequent pauses between words thus creating an environment that meets the description for obstruent devoicing in German and prevents across-the-word voice assimilation that is pervasive in Slovak. Additionally, the presence of these pauses facilitates so called pre-boundary lengthening (e.g. Delattre, 1968 for German), in which the rime of the pre-pausal syllable is elongated. Finally, a generally slower rate may result in vowels intended as short to be perceived as long especially in the speech that is slowed down locally (for example with unknown words for L2 speakers).

4 ASR experiment

The analysis of accent sentences in the previous section revealed a potential impact of slower speaking rate of L2 speakers on the frequency of pronunciation deviations. We test the effects of speaking rate and variability in the pronunciation dictionary on the recognition of German accented Slovak in the following experiment.

4.1 Test setup

The training audio database contained 130 hours of phonetically rich sentences, gender balanced, from domains such as news and articles from various magazines, recorded from 140 speakers with Sennheiser ME3 headset microphone with Sennheiser MZA 900 P in-line preamplifier and EMU Tracker Pre USB audio interface. Database was annotated using the Transcriber annotation tool (Barras et al., 2000), twice checked and corrected. Recordings were split on segments if possible not bigger than 10 sec.

The training text corpora contained a total of about 92 million sentences with 1.25 billion Slovak words. A general-domain trigram language model (LM) was created with a vocabulary size of 350k unique words (400k pronunciation variants) which passed the spell-check lexicon and subsequently were also checked manually. Similarly to other recognizers in Slovak (Staš, Hládek and Juhár, 2010) the modified Kneser-Ney algorithm was used as a smoothing technique. The general LM was adapted with all 590 sentences from the target domain.

The Julius decoder (Lee, Kawahara, and Shikano, 2001) was used as a reference speech recognition engine, and the HTK toolkit was used for word-internal acoustic models (AMs) training. We trained AMs using the triphone mapping as described in (Darjaa et al., 2011), with 32 Gaussian densities per each HMM state.

Experiments have been performed using AMs and LM trained from the training databases, and the 8010 sentences from the testing corpus as described in Section 2.

4.2 Results

To estimate the potential effect of slow L2 speech on the recognition accuracy, we first performed signal level acceleration directly on the recorded waveforms. The Praat speech analysis system (Boersma and Weenink 2011) was used, particularly its functionality of adjusting the time-domain of a sound file with a fixed conversion factor used in subsequent PSOLA resynthesis of the resulting file. We resynthesized all test sentences using the factors 0.9, 0.7, and 0.5 (the last one corresponding to 50% duration of the original file) and performed recognition with an unadapted LM that had the baseline WER of 55%. The results showed that the acceleration factor with the highest accuracy gain was 0.7, which improved the baseline to 43.4% WER. Factor 0.9 lowered WER to 49.5% while factor 0.5 showed the worst result (54.1% WER).

Following this encouraging initial result, feature level acceleration was performed by simple change of frame shift in the ASR front-end. The original features were calculated from 25 ms frame durations and a 10 ms frame shift. While keeping the frame durations constant, we increased the frame shift to 14 ms. This corresponds to the acceleration factor of 0.714, approximately identical to the best performing factor in the signal modulation experiments.

Table 2 shows achieved recognition results based on the adapted LM used as the baseline. This refers to the performance of the system on German accent sentences without any rate modifications. Unfortunately, we don't have a corpus of these sentences produced by Slovak speakers to provide a system baseline for non-accented speech but in a similar, albeit larger, corpus of 18 speakers reading 380 sentences this system's WER was 21.3% (Beňuš et al., 2011).

Speaker rate was accelerated at the signal and feature levels. We see that both signal and feature adaptation of speech rate significantly improved the accuracy of recognition with the latter outperforming the former. The extent of the improvement is rather surprising and suggests that speech rate in read sentences is a major factor when recognizing German-accented Slovak.

Test	**WER %**
Baseline	40.58
Alternate dictionary	40.48
Signal-adapted speech rate	28.67
Signal-adapted rate+alt. dictionary	28.13
Feature-adapted speech rate	25.79
Feature-adapted rate+alt. dictionary	25.33

Table 2: Word error rates (WER) for signal and feature adaptations (speech rate accelerations).

The analysis in section 3 also identified two common patterns: devoicing of consonants of German speakers that, in regular fluent Slovak, would be produced as voiced, and vowel shortening of German speakers. We tried to use this knowledge for improving the speech recognition system. In order to better match the pronunciation of German speakers in Slovak ASR system, we added alternative pronunciations to each entry of Slovak dictionary according to Table 3. For example, the entry 'Aachene' with pronunciation /a: x e J e/, was extended with an alternative pronunciation /a x e n e/ by the application of the rules in the 1st and 4th rows.

Original phones	**Phones used in alternative pronunciations**
/J/, /n/	/n/
/c/, /t/	/t/
/J\/, /d/	/d/
/a:/ /e:/ /i:/ /o:/ /u:/	/a/, /e/, /i/, /o/, /u/

Table 3: Rules for generation of alternative pronunciations (/J/, /c/, /J\/ are Slovak SAMPA symbols for palatal variants of /n/, /t/, and /d/ respectively).

The results in Table 2 show that the changes to the dictionary resulted in only insignificant improvements on top of the rate adjustment.

Finally, we compared the average WER for individual speakers in the baseline system with the adapted systems. For 17 out of 18 speakers the improvement was greater than 5% and ranged up to 34%; only one speaker's results showed deterioration (2%). Interestingly, despite a relatively good correspondence between the proficiency level and the number of pronunciation errors showed in Figure 1, neither the recognition accuracy of the adapted model, nor the extent of improvement after feature adaptation, showed a consistent relationship to the perceived proficiency of our subjects. This may be due to the greater number and complexity of test sentences used for advanced speakers compared to the beginners.

5 Discussion and conclusion

Our results showed that adjusting the rate of non-native speech to resemble the rate of the native training corpus significantly improves the recognition of speech with foreign accent. Moreover, we showed that feature-based acceleration outperforms signal-based acceleration. This is important since feature-based acceleration is much easier to perform, and an ASR system runs faster as it processes less frames. Furthermore, it is plausible that speech rate variability will be similar in non-native accents of multiple L1 languages, which cannot be expected for the pronunciation variants. Hence, although the acceleration of the signal or features does not account for all of the phonetic interference phenomena described in Section 3.2, sophisticated speech rate modeling that includes the combination of phone rate, syllable rate, and word rate promises to provide a robust technique for dealing with variability stemming from non-native accents.

6 Acknowledgments

This work was supported by the European Project of Structural Funds, ITMS: 26240220064.

References

Barras, C., Geoffrois, E., Wu, Z., and Liberman, M. 2000. Transcriber: development and use of a tool for assisting speech corpora production. Speech Communication, 33 (1–2).

Beňuš, Š., Cerňak, M., Rusko, M., Trnka, M., Darjaa, S., and Sabo, R. 2011. Semi-automatic approach to ASR errors categorization in multi-speaker corpora. *Proceedings of the International Conference Slovko.*

Beňuš, Š, and Mády, K. 2010. Effects of lexical stress and speech rate on the quantity and quality of Slovak vowels. *Proceedings of the 5th International Conference on Speech Prosody.*

Boersma, P., and Weenink, D. 2011. Praat: doing phonetics by computer [Computer program, http://www.praat.org/].

Darjaa, S., Cerňak, M., Trnka, M., Rusko, M., Sabo, R. 2011. Effective Triphone Mapping for Acoustic Modeling in Speech Recognition. *Proceedings of Interspeech 2011 Conference.*

Delattre, P. 1968. A Comparison of Syllable Length Conditioning Among Languages. *International Review of Applied Linguistics*, IV:183-198.

Gusfield, D.. 1997. Algorithms on Strings, Trees and Sequences. Cambridge University Press, Cambridge, UK.

Lee, A., Kawahara, T., and Shikano, K. 2001. Julius – an Open Source Real-Time Large Vocabulary Recognition Engine. In *Proc. of the European Conference on Speech Communications and Technology (EUROSPEECH).*

Oh, Y.R., Yoon, J.S., Kim, H.K. 2007. Acoustic model adaptation based on pronunciation variability analysis for non-native speech recognition. Speech Communication 49(1), 59-70.

Staš, J., Hládek, D., Juhár, J. 2010. Language Model Adaptation for Slovak LVCSR. In *Proc. of the Intl. Conference on AEI*, pp. 101–106.

Tomokiyo, L.M., 2000. Lexical and acoustic modeling of non-native speech in LVCSR. In: Proc. ICSLP, Beijing, China, pp. 346–349.

Phone set selection for HMM-based dialect speech synthesis

Michael Pucher
Telecommunications
Research Center (FTW)
Vienna, Austria
pucher@ftw.at

Nadja Kerschhofer-Puhalo
Acoustics Research
Institute (ARI)
Vienna, Austria
nadja.kerschhofer@oeaw.ac.at

Dietmar Schabus
Telecommunications
Research Center (FTW)
Vienna, Austria
schabus@ftw.at

Abstract

This paper describes a method for selecting an appropriate phone set in dialect speech synthesis for a so far undescribed dialect by applying hidden Markov model (HMM) based training and clustering methods. In this pilot study we show how a phone set derived from the phonetic surface can be optimized given a small amount of dialect speech training data.

1 Introduction

In acoustic modeling for dialect speech synthesis we are confronted with two closely related major problems[1], (1) to find an appropriate phone set for synthesis and (2) to design a recording script with sufficient phonetic and prosodic coverage. In HMM-based synthesis, we can use the training process of the voices itself to analyze the used phone set and to try to optimize it for synthesis.

2 Corpus and phone set design

Goiserian, the dialect of Bad Goisern in the most southern part of Upper Austria, is a local dialect of the Middle Bavarian/Southern Bavarian transition zone. The target variety for speech synthesis described here demonstrates the typical problems related to scarcity of data. While several varieties of the central and northern part of Upper Austria are quite well described, detailed descriptions of the varieties in this region do not exist. Lacking a lexicon, a phonological description, orthographic rules or a transcription system, a speech corpus and an appropriate phone set have to be created. Our current project aims at audio-visual dialect synthesis, which is based on a systematic description of speech data collected from spontaneous speech, word lists and translated sentences by 10 speakers of the same dialect. Although it would be ideal to use conversational speech data for dialect speech synthesis (Campbell, 2006) we decided to use a hybrid approach for our full corpus where we plan to collect a set of prompts from conversational dialect speech, which will be realized by the dialect speakers.

The speech data for the first preliminary study presented here consists of 150 sentences and colloquial phrases spoken in Goiserian by a female speaker who can be described as a conservative speaker of the original basic dialect of the region. The prompts were translated spontaneously by the speaker from Standard German into Goiserian and contain typical phonetic and phonological characteristics of local Bavarian varieties in multiple occurrences.

3 Voice building

The data was originally recorded at 96kHz, 24 bit and was downsampled to 16kHz, 16 bit for synthesis and voice building. A preliminary phone set (PS1) was created on the basis of a fine phonetic transcription including sub-phonemic details (e.g. nasalization of vowels before nasals "VN"). Phones occurring less than twice were substituted prior to voice training with phonetically similar phones or representatives of the same phoneme. This leaves us with a set of 72 phones (see Table 1 and 2).

[1]Apart from additional problems that have to do with text analysis, orthography, and grapheme-to-phoneme conversion.

Proceedings of EMNLP 2011, Conference on Empirical Methods in Natural Language Processing, pages 65–69,
Edinburgh, Scotland, UK, July 27–31, 2011. ©2011 Association for Computational Linguistics

The TRA voice was trained with a HMM-based speaker-dependent system. Given the limited amount of training data (150 prompts) and to be able to analyze the decision trees we only used the current, 2 preceding, and 2 succeeding phones as features.

HTK	IPA	#	HTK	IPA	#
s	s	207	t	t	204
d	d	179	n	n	171
m	m	115	k	k	98
h	h	84	g	g	79
v	v	79	f	f	62
r	r	61	S	ʃ	49
N	n̩	42	l	l	41
b	b	31	ts	ts	27
ng	ŋ	19	p	p	17
w	β	14	L	l̩	12
X	x	11	c	c	10
RX	χ	9	j	j	7
R	ɾ	6	ks	ks	3
pf	pf	3			

Table 1: Consonants (27) in phone set PS1 for training (72 phones) (Blue = not in PS2).

Based on a phonetic transcription of the training corpus, flat-start forced alignment with HTK was carried out. Stops are split into two parts, one for the closure and one for plosion plus burst. Additionally, we applied forced alignment using pronunciation variants[2], which is the preferred method when building a voice for dialect synthesis using a larger corpus (Pucher, 2010). With this method it is not necessary to have a phonetic transcription of the recordings. Given our small corpus, this method produced several errors ([tsvoa] / [tsvai], [tsum] / [tsun] etc.) which led us to use the standard alignment method from a transcription of the corpus. After the transcription we had to correct severe alignment errors. These errors are simple to find since several segments within the utterance are affected.

From this corpus we selected 5 prompts containing only phonemes that appear at least more than 3 times in the rest of the corpus. This leaves us with a training corpus of 145 prompts and a 5 prompt test set. For the subjective evaluation, the entire resynthesized corpus was used to show us how well the used phone set covers the data.

HTK	IPA	#	HTK	IPA	#
a	a	138	aa	aː	10
A	ɒ	80	AA	ɒː	3
AN	ɒ̃	80	Ai	ɒi	3
AuN	ɒ̃u	7			
e	e	100	ee	eː	9
ei	ei	22	eiN	ẽi	10
E	ɛ	20	EE	ɛː	11
EN	ɛ̃	4	EiN	ɛ̃i	6
i	i	175	ii	iː	7
iN	ĩ	6			
o	o	45	oo	oː	3
ou	ou	4	Ou	ɔ	4
u	u	20	U	ʊ	15
UN	ʊ̃	3			
q	ø	9	qY	øʏ	3
QY	œʏ	4			
y	y	9	yy	yː	3
Y	ʏ	4			
eV	ə	11	aV	ɐ	89
ai	ai	24	aiN	ãi	9
au	au	24	ea	eɐ	7
eaN	ẽɐ	4	ia	iɐ	30
oa	oɐ	16	oaN	õɐ	9
Oi	ɔi	6	oi	oi	26
ua	uɐ	21	ui	ui	6

Table 2: Vowels (33) and diphtongs (12) in phone set PS1 for training (72 phones) (Blue = not in PS2, Red = not in PS2 and PS3, green = not in PS3).

The 145 prompts were then used for training a speaker-dependent HMM-based synthetic voice. Figure 1 shows the architecture of the HMM-based speaker dependent system (Zen, 2005). For synthesis we used the full-context label files of the corpus without duration information. By that text analysis is not necessary for synthesis. Our implicit assumption is that the letter-to-sound rules and text analysis produce exactly the string of phones from the transcription. In this way we can evaluate the acoustic modeling part separately, independently from text analysis.

[2]In a previous project on Viennese dialect synthesis, 33% of the lexicon entries are pronunciation variants.

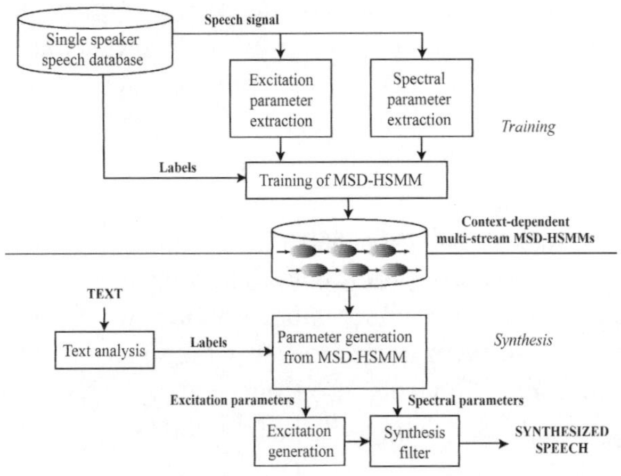

Figure 1: HMM-based speaker dependent speech synthesis system.

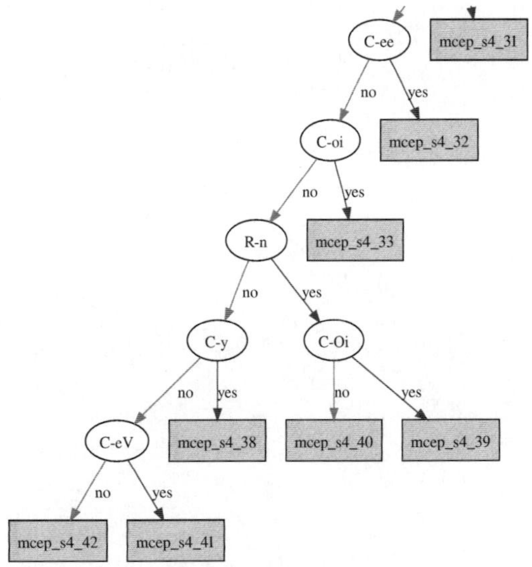

Figure 2: Part of the mel-cepstrum clustering tree for the 3rd state of the HMM.

4 Voice analysis

To be able to analyze the decision trees we used phone features only. The HMM-based voice consists of a mel-cepstrum, duration, F0, and an aperiodicity model. In a first step we defined the phones that are not used for modeling, or are used for a certain model only.

Figure 3 shows those phones that are not used for clustering of the different models. This may be due to their rare occurrence in the data (3-4 times) or due to possible inconsistencies in their phonetic realization. The F0 model is not shown since all phonemes were used in the F0 tree in some context.

To define other possible phone sets we decided to substitute the phones only occurring in the F0 model but not in the other 3 models, namely the mel-cepstrum, duration, and the aperiodicity model. We therefore merged "Ai", "AuN", "EN", "ks", "L", "Ou", "qY", "yy" with their phonetically most similar equivalents (e.g. syllabic "L" with "l", "ks" with "k"+"s", or a nasalized "EN" or "AuN" before nasals with the non-nasal phone) and thus obtained a new smaller phone set (PS2), which was used for training a second voice model.

Another possible set of phones (PS 3) is defined by merging long (VV) and short (V) vowels of the same quality, namely "ii", "yy", "ee", "EE", "aa", "AA", "oo" with their short counterpart. From a linguistic point of view, the phonemic status of vowel duration as a primary feature in Austrian German is a controversial issue. While differences in length do exist at the phonetic surface, these differences are not necessarily of phonemic relevance (Moosmüller, 2007; Scheutz, 1985). We obtain thus a third phone set (PS3) by merging long and short vowels.

Model	#	#C	#L	#LL	#R	#RR
Mel-cep.	42	38	2	0	1	0
Aperiod.	36	31	0	3	0	1
F0	196	54	37	38	30	36
Duration	83	32	14	9	14	13

Table 3: Number of models and questions in mel-cepstrum, aperiodicity, F0, and duration model for central HMM state.

4.1 Mel-cepstrum and aperiodicity model

The mel-cepstrum model contains a separate model for each phone that is used in the cepstral clustering. In Figure 2 this is shown with the model "mcep_s4_32", which is used in case that the current phone is an "ee" (C-ee) and with the model "mcep_s4_33", which is used in case that the current phone is an "oi". These two models are special models which only cover certain phones. The only effect of the clustering is that some phones are not modeled separately, resulting in an unbalanced tree.

However there is one instance of context cluster-

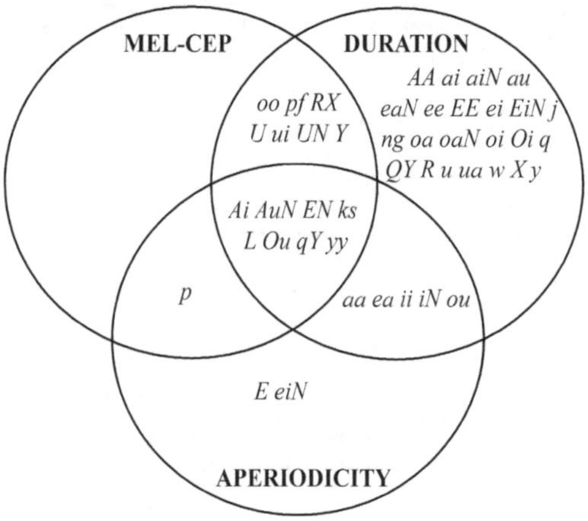

Figure 3: Phones that were not used for clustering in the trees for mel-cepstrum, duration, and aperiodicity in any context (current, 2 preceding, and 2 succeeding phones) and any of the 5 states.

ing in the central state of the mel-cepstrum HMMs. If the right phone is an "n" (R-n) there are two different models used ("mcep_s4_39", "mcep_s4_40"), depending on whether the current phone is an "Oi" (C-Oi) or not (Figure 2).

All phones that are not modeled through a separate model are modeled by the model at the end of the tree (model "mcep_s4_42").

The aperiodicity model is very similar to the mel-cepstrum model, as can be seen in Table 3 and Figure 3.

4.2 F0 and duration model

The F0 model uses all phones as shown in Figure 3 and is the most complex model in terms of context questions as can be seen from Table 3.

The duration model contains the lowest number of phone related questions as shown by Figure 3 but is still more complex than the spectrum related models in terms of context-dependent questions as shown in Table 3. Similarly to the F0 model, it is rather difficult to analyze this model directly.

5 Voice evaluation

After the analysis of the voice that was trained with our basic phoneset PS1 we defined two new phonesets PS2 and PS3. These phonesets were used to train additional voice models for the same speaker. With these voice models, we synthesized our small set of 5 test sentences. To evaluate the suitability of the phonesets for the training data, we re-synthesized the training corpus of 145 prompts.

In a pair-wise comparison test of the 150 prompts we evaluated the three voice models in a subjective listening test with three expert listeners. The experts listened to a set of prompts, each prompt synthesized with two different voice models. They were asked to compare them and to decide which prompt they would prefer in terms of overall quality, or whether they would rate them as "equally good".

PS1	PS2	PS3
56	102	105

Table 4: Number of winning comparisons per phone set (PS1-PS3).

Table 4 illustrates that both approaches to reduce and redefine the phoneset (PS2, PS3) improved the overall quality estimation considerably compared to the initial phoneset PS1.

6 Conclusion

One major challenge for speech synthesis of so far undescribed varieties is the lack of an appropriate phoneset and sufficient training data. We met this challenge by deriving a phoneset directly from the phonetic surface of a very restricted corpus of natural speech. This phone set was used for voice training. Based on the outcome of the first voice training we reconsidered the choice of phones and created new phone sets following 2 approaches: (1) removing phones that are not used in the clustering, and (2) a linguistically motivated choice of phone substitutions based on clustering results. Both methods yielded a considerable improvement of voice quality. Thus, HMM-based machine learning methods and supervised optimization can be used for the definition of the phoneset of an unkown dialect. Our future work will elaborate this method with dialect speech training corpora of different size to show whether it can be applied to adaptive methods involving multiple-speaker training. The consideration of inter- and intra-speaker variation and style shifting will be a crucial question for further study.

References

Nick Campbell. 2006. *Conversational speech synthesis and the need for some laughter.* IEEE Transactions on Speech and Audio Processing, 14(4), pages 1171-1178.

Michael Pucher, Friedrich Neubarth, Volker Strom, Sylvia Moosmüller, Gregor Hofer, Christian Kranzler, Gudrun Schuchmann and Dietmar Schabus. 2010. *Resources for speech synthesis of Viennese varieties.* In Proceedings of the 7th International Conference on Language Resources and Evaluation (LREC), Valletta, Malta.

Sylvia Moosmüller. 2007. *Vowels in Standard Austrian German. An Acoustic-Phonetic and Phonological Analysis.* Habilitationsschrift, Vienna.

Hannes Scheutz. 1985. *Strukturen der Lautveränderung.* Braumüller, Vienna.

Heiga Zen and Tomoki Toda. 2005. *An Overview of Nitech HMM-based Speech Synthesis System for Blizzard Challenge 2005.* In Proceedings of the 9th European Conference on Speech Communication and Technology (INTERSPEECH), Lisboa, Portugal.

WordNet.PT$_{global}$ – Extending WordNet.PT to Portuguese varieties

Palmira Marrafa[1], Raquel Amaro[2] and Sara Mendes[2]
Group for the Computation of Lexical and Grammatical Knowledge,
Center of Linguistics of the University of Lisbon
Avenida Professor Gama Pinto, 2
1649-003 Lisboa, Portugal
[1]palmira.marrafa@netcabo.pt [2]{ramaro,sara.mendes}@clul.ul.pt

Abstract

This paper reports the results of the WordNet.PT$_{global}$ project, an extension of WordNet.PT to all Portuguese varieties. Profiting from a theoretical model of high level explanatory adequacy and from a convenient and flexible development tool, WordNet.PT$_{global}$ achieves a rich and multi-purpose lexical resource, suitable for contrastive studies and for a vast range of language-based applications covering all Portuguese varieties.

1 Introduction

WordNet.PT is being built since July 1999, at the Center of Linguistics of the University of Lisbon as a project developed by the *Group for the Computation of Lexical and Grammatical Knowledge* (CLG).

WordNet.PT is being developed within the general approach of EuroWordNet (Vossen 1998, 1999). Therefore, like each wordnet in EWN, WordNet.PT has a general conceptual architecture structured along the lines of the Princeton WordNet (Miller *et al.* 1990; Fellbaum 1998).

For early strategic reasons concerning applications, this project is being carried out on the basis of manual work, assuring the accuracy and reliability of its results.

Aiming at using the Portuguese WordNet in language learning applications, among others, the starting point for the specification of a fragment of the Portuguese lexicon, in the first phase of the project (1999-2003), consisted in the selection of a set of semantic domains covering concepts with high productivity in daily life communication. The encoding of language-internal relations followed a mixed top-down/bottom-up strategy for the extension of small local nets (Marrafa 2002). Such work firstly focused on nouns, but has since then been extended to all the main POS, a work which has resulted both in refining information specifications and increasing WordNet.PT coverage (Amaro *et al.* 2006; Marrafa *et al.* 2006; Amaro 2009; Mendes 2009).

Relational lexica, and wordnets in particular, play a leading role in machine lexical knowledge representation. Hence, providing Portuguese with such a rich linguistic resource, and particularly Portuguese varieties not often considered in lexical resources, is crucial, not only to researchers working in contrastive studies or with the so-called non-standard varieties, but also to the general public, as the database is made available for consultation in the WWW through an intuitive and perspicuous web interface. Such work is also particularly relevant as the resulting database can be extensively used in a vast range of language-based applications, able to cover, this way, all Portuguese varieties.

This paper depicts the work developed and the results achieved under the scope of the WordNet.PT$_{global}$ project, funded by Instituto Camões, which, as mentioned above, aims at extending WordNet.PT to Portuguese varieties.

Proceedings of EMNLP 2011, Conference on Empirical Methods in Natural Language Processing, pages 70–74,
Edinburgh, Scotland, UK, July 27–31, 2011. ©2011 Association for Computational Linguistics

2 The Data

Portuguese is spoken in all five continents by over 250 million speakers, according to recent studies, and is the official language of 8 countries: Angola, Brazil, Cape Verde, East Timor, Guinea Bissau, Mozambique, Portugal, and Sao Tome e Principe. Being spoken in geographically distant regions and by very different communities, both in terms of size and culture, Portuguese is naturally expected to show variation. Despite this, regional varieties are far from being equally provided with linguistic resources representing their specificities, as most research work is focused either on the Brazilian or the European varieties[1].

In the work depicted here we aim at contributing to reverse this situation, considering that this kind of resource is particularly adequate to achieve this goal, since it allows for representing lexical variation in a very straightforward way: concepts are the basic unit in wordnets, defined by a set of lexical conceptual relations with other concepts, and represented by the set of lexical expressions (tendentially all) that denote them. We have to antecipate the possibility of different varieties showing distinct lexicalization patterns, particularly some lexical gaps or lexicalizations of more specific concepts. This is straightforwardly dealt with in the WordNet model: once a system of relevant tags has been implemented in the database in order to identify lexical expressions with regard to their corresponding varieties, lexical gaps are simply encoded by not associating the tag of the variety at stake to any of the variants in the synset; specific lexicalizations, on the other hand, are added to the network as a new node and associated to the variety tag at stake.

Our approach consisted in extracting 10 000 concepts from WordNet.PT, and associating them with the lexical expressions that denote them in each Portuguese variety considered in this project. In order to accomplish this, we consulted native speakers from each of these varieties, resident in their original communities, and asked them to pinpoint the expressions used for denoting the aforementioned 10 000 concepts. Informants were selected by Instituto Camões among undergrad students in Portuguese studies and supervised by Portuguese lectors in each local university. Besides the European Portuguese variety, which is already encoded in WordNet.PT, specifications for six other Portuguese varieties were integrated in the database [2] : Angolan Portuguese, Brazilian Portuguese, Cape Verdean Portuguese, East Timorese Portuguese, Mozambican Portuguese and Sao Tome e Principe Portuguese. For each concept, several lexicalizations were identified and both the marked and unmarked expressions regarding usage information[3] were considered and identified.

2.1 Data selection

As mentioned above, our approach for enriching WordNet.PT with lexicalizations from all Portuguese varieties consisted in extracting 10 000 concepts from WordNet.PT and associating them to the lexical expressions which denote them in each variety.

domain	**nouns**	**verbs**	**adjectives**	**proper nouns**	**total**
art	422	14	83	0	519
clothes	467	62	74	0	603
communication	314	151	106	82	653
education	536	37	30	82	685
food	1131	130	115	0	1376
geography	281	0	166	200	647
health	1159	92	175	0	1426
housing	595	28	46	0	669
human activities	641	0	0	0	641
human relations	620	189	100	0	909
living things	1597	113	119	1	1830
sports	480	34	23	2	539
transportation	659	562	67	30	659
all domains	7893	802	1022	284	10001
domain overlap	10,36%	12,54%	4,22%	22,62%	10,35%

Table 1: concepts extended to Portuguese varieties

[1] Official standardized versions of East Timorese and African varieties of Portuguese essentially correspond to that of European Portuguese. Moreover, these varieties are not provided with dedicated lexical resources, such as dictionaries or large-scale corpora. Being so, speakers in these regions generally use European Portuguese lexical resources, which only exceptionally cover lexical variants specific to these varieties.

[2] All Portuguese varieties spoken in countries where Portuguese is the official language were considered. However, for the time being, data from Guinean Portuguese are not yet encoded in the WordNet.PT_{global} database due to difficulties in maintaining a regular contact with the native speakers consulted. Despite this, we still hope to be able to include this variety in the database at some point in the future.

[3] Informants were provided with a limited inventory of usage markers: slang; vulgar; informal; humerous; popular; unusual; regional; technical; old-fashioned.

The semantic domain approach initially used in developing WordNet.PT, provided us with a natural starting point for the selection of data to be considered in this project. The table above presents the distribution, per POS and semantic domain[4], of the WordNet.PT concepts extended to non-European Portuguese varieties.

2.2 Data implementation

Once the data described above were presented to the native speakers consulted and their input organized, all the information obtained was incorporated in the database.

This way, for a concept like ***bus*** (public transportation which has regular pre-established stops at short intervals, typically operating within cities), for instance, the following lexicalizations were obtained: *autocarro*, *machibombo*, *machimbombo*, *ônibus*, and *microônibus*. *Autocarro* was found to be the more common expression used for denoting the concept at stake in Angola, Cape Verde, East Timor, Portugal, Sao Tome e Principe and Mozambique. However, this variant is marked as "unusual" in Mozambique variety. *Machibombo* and *machimbombo* are only used in Mozambique, whereas *ônibus* and *microônibus* are only used in Brazil. With this kind of data at hand, each lexicalization was tagged with regard to the varieties in which it is used and, for each variety, associated, when relevant, to a usage label, as illustrated below.

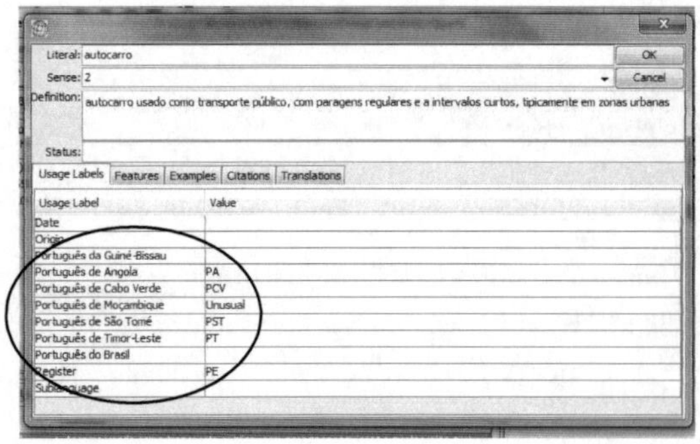

In the codification of the aforementioned information we used ***Synsetter*** – a new, very flexible wordnet development tool previously developed for the full implementation of innovative research results in WordNet.PT. In order to do so, this computational tool has been developed to straightforwardly allow for updates and improvements. In the specific case of the task addressed in this paper, extending the coverage of the WordNet.PT database to lexicalizations of different Portuguese varieties involved the design of additional features regarding the identification of Portuguese varieties and variety-dependent usage label encoding.

2.3 The results

Encoding the data obtained in WordNet.PT$_{global}$ extends a relevant fragment of WordNet.PT to Portuguese varieties other than European Portuguese. This way, researchers are provided with a crucial database for developing contrastive studies on the lexicon of different Portuguese varieties or research on a specific Portuguese variety, just to mention a possible application. The table below presents the distribution of variants per variety in the fragment of the lexicon considered, making apparent, for instance, that in the collection of data considered in this project some varieties have more synonym forms for denoting the same concept than others (see average of variants per concept).

Portuguese varieties	**number of concepts**	**number of variants**	**variants per concept (average)**
Angola	10 000	11713	1,17
Brazil	10 000	12060	1,20
Cape Verde	10 000	12563	1,26
East Timor	10 000	12131	1,21
Mozambique	10 000	11740	1,17
Portugal	10 000	13006	1,30
Sao Tome e Principe	6981	9552	1,37
all varieties	10 000	14751	1,47

Naturally, this is only an overall view of the results obtained. The new extended WordNet.PT version is also a crucial resource allowing for contrastive studies on lexicalization patterns depending on semantic domains or on frequency of use, for instance, for all or for specific Portuguese varieties.

In order to make these data publicly available, a new WordNet.PT version, the WordNet.PT$_{global}$ has been released on the WWW[5]. Releasing the WordNet.PT fragment extended to Portuguese

[4] Note that some of the concepts considered are associated to more than one semantic domain. This results in partial overlaps between semantic domains, whose extent is presented in the last row of Table 1.

[5] http://www.clul.ul.pt/wnglobal.

varieties online involved developing an updated version of the web interface for wordnet online navigation. In Section 3 we present the main features of this web interface and how users can navigate and straightforwardly access the data on Portuguese varieties.

3 Navigating the lexicon of Portuguese varieties online

The new updated version of the web interface for wordnet navigation was developed with specific features allowing for the visualization of information on Portuguese varieties and for narrowing down searches depending on the needs of the user. Among the most salient aspects of the new web interface we underline the following: allowing the user to restrict the search to a given (or to a set of) Portuguese variety(ies) (see caption below); displaying information about each lexical expression regarding the varieties which use it and whether this use is marked or not.

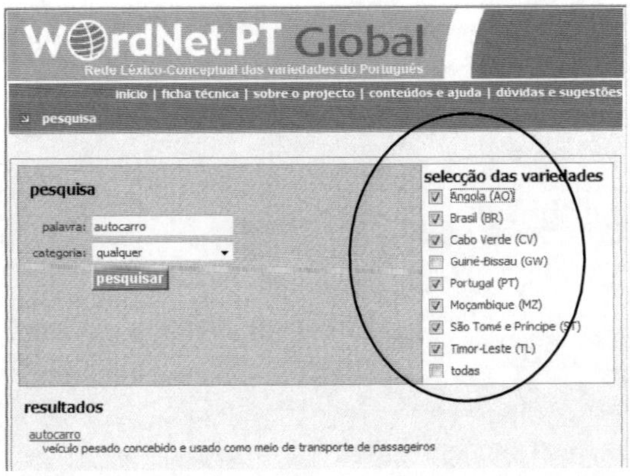

Going back to the example mentioned in section 2.2, in Portuguese, the concept {**bus**} can be denoted by several expressions, depending on the variety considered. This information is straightforwardly displayed and made available to the user by a simple system of tags, as illustrated below.

Also, all marked uses are indicated by underlining the variety label corresponding to the variety in which the use of the relevant expression is marked (see tags associated to *autocarro* in the caption above, particularly the *MZ* tag signaled by an arrow). By clicking on this label the relevant usage label is displayed, as illustrated below.

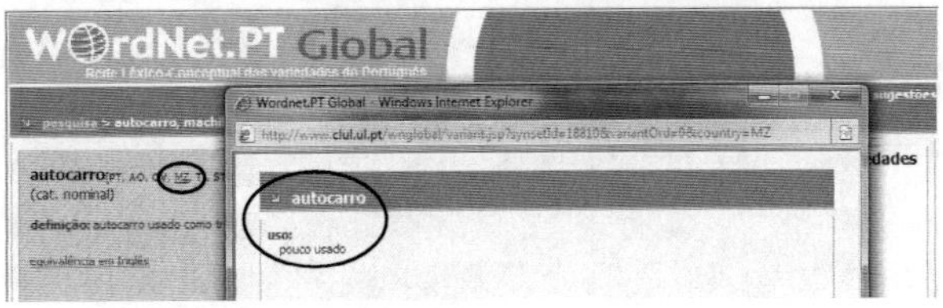

4 Final Remarks

WordNet.PT_{global} is, thus, a relational lexicon allowing for modelling the lexicon of Portuguese varieties in a consistent and motivated way.

Covering 10 000 concepts, lexicalized by a total of 14 751 expressions representing all the main POS (nouns, verbs, adjectives, and proper nouns), WordNet.PT_{global} also provides a lexical-conceptual network of relations establishing the relevant links between each concept and the other concepts in the net, in a total of more than 30 000 relations, including relations with their corresponding lexicalizations in English.

This way, Portuguese now has a rich and useful lexical resource covering all of its varieties (Angolan, Brazilian, Cape Verdean, East Timorese, European, Mozambican, Sao Tome e Principe and Guinean Portuguese (forthcoming – see footnote 1)), freely available for online consultation both to researchers and to the general public.

Moreover, the database presented in this paper can be extensively used in a vast range of language-based applications which are now able to cover all Portuguese varieties. As a final remark on future work, the data resulting from WordNet.PT_{global} can be used as a basis for comparative studies regarding, for instance, variant distribution per variety. Note, however, that pursuing such studies requires comparable corpora for each variety, both with POS tagging and semantic annotation. Nonetheless, several advances are being taken in this direction[6].

[6] see http://www.clul.ul.pt/en/research-teams/87-linguistic-resources-for-the-study-of-the-african-varieties-of-portuguese-r.

References

Amaro, R. (2009) *Computation of Verbal Predicates in Portuguese: relational network, lexical-conceptual structure and context – the case of verbs of movement*, PhD dissertation, University of Lisbon.

Amaro, R., R. P. Chaves, P. Marrafa & S. Mendes (2006) "Enriching WordNets with new relations and with event and argument structures", *Proceedings of CICLing 2006*, Mexico City, pp. 28-40.

Fellbaum, C. (1998) (ed.) *WordNet: an Electronic Lexical Database*, MA: The MIT Press.

Marrafa, P. (2002) "The Portuguese WordNet: General Architecture and Semantic Internal Relations", *DELTA*, Brasil.

Marrafa, P., R. Amaro, R. P. Chaves, S. Lourosa & S. Mendes (2006) "WordNet.PT new directions", *Proceedings of GWC'06*, Jeju Island, pp. 319-321.

Mendes, S. (2009) *Syntax and Semantics of Adjectives in Portuguese: analysis and modelling*, PhD dissertation, University of Lisbon.

Miller, G., R. Beckwith, C. Fellbaum, D. Gross & K. J. Miller (1990) "Introduction to WordNet: An On-line Lexical Database", *International Journal of Lexicography*, volume 3, number 4.

Vossen, P. (1998) (ed.) *EuroWordNet: A Multilingual Database with Lexical Semantic Networks*, Dordrecht: Kluwer Academic Publishers.

Vossen, P. (1999) *EuroWordNet General Document*, University of Amsterdam.

Author Index

Association for Computational Linguistics
209 N. Eighth Street
Stroudsburg, Pennsylvania 18360

CURRAN ASSOCIATES INC
proceedings.com